Ravensong

ALSO BY CATHERINE FEHER-ELSTON

Wolfsong: A Natural and Fabulous History of Wolves

RavenSong

A NATURAL AND FABULOUS HISTORY OF RAVENS AND CROWS

by Catherine Feher-Elston
Illustrated by Lawrence Ormsby

JEREMY P. TARCHER / PENGUIN
a member of Penguin Group (USA) Inc.
New York

JEREMY P. TARCHER/PENGUIN
Published by the Penguin Group
www.penguin.com
Penguin Group (USA) Inc., 375 Hudson Street, New York, New York 10014, USA
Penguin Group (Canada), 10 Alcorn Avenue, Toronto, Ontario M4V 3B2, Canada
(a division of Pearson Penguin Canada Inc.)
Penguin Books Ltd, 80 Strand, London WC2R 0RL, England
Penguin Ireland, 25 St Stephen's Green, Dublin 2, Ireland (a division of Penguin Books Ltd)
Penguin Group (Australia), 250 Camberwell Road, Camberwell, Victoria 3124, Australia
(a division of Pearson Australia Group Pty Ltd)
Penguin Books India Pvt Ltd, 11 Community Centre, Panchsheel Park, New Delhi–110 017, India
Penguin Group (NZ), Cnr Airborne and Rosedale Roads, Albany, Auckland 1310, New Zealand
(a division of Pearson New Zealand Ltd)
Penguin Books (South Africa) (Pty) Ltd, 24 Sturdee Avenue, Rosebank, Johannesburg 2196,
South Africa

Penguin Books Ltd, Registered Offices: 80 Strand, London WC2R 0RL, England

First Jeremy P. Tarcher edition 2005
Copyright © 1991, 2004 by Catherine Feher-Elston
Illustrations © 1991 by Lawrence Ormsby

Most Tarcher/Penguin books are available at special quantity discounts for bulk purchase for sales
promotions, premiums, fund-raising, and educational needs. Special books or book excerpts also
can be created to fit specific needs. For details, write Penguin Group (USA) Inc. Special Markets,
375 Hudson Street, New York, NY 10014.

Library of Congress Cataloging-in-Publication Data

Feher-Elston, Catherine, date.
    Ravensong : a natural and fabulous history of ravens and crows / by Catherine Feher-Elston ;
illustrated by Lawrence Ormsby.
        p. cm.
    Originally published: Flagstaff, AZ : Northland Pub., © 1991. With new introductory note.
    Includes bibliographical references and index.
    ISBN 1-58542-357-2
    1. Ravens—Folklore.   2. Crows—Folklore.   3. Ravens—History.   4. Crows—History.
5. Indians of North America—Northwest, Pacific—Folklore.   6. Indian mythology—
Northwest, Pacific.   I. Title.
    GR735.F44   2004   2004058838
    398'.3698864—dc22

Printed in the United States of America
10 9 8 7 6 5 4 3 2 1

This book is printed on acid-free paper. ∞

Book design by Carole Thickstun

For Gagee, Wimi, Crowsey,

and the Bird People

Contents

Make prayers to the Raven.
Raven that is,
Raven that was,
Raven that always will be.
Make prayers to the Raven.
Raven, bring us luck.

FROM THE KOYUKON

This is the story about crows:
One is for sorrow.
Two is for mirth.
Three is a wedding.
Four is a birth.

FROM AN OLD AMERICAN RHYME

Acknowledgments

The past year has been a kind of corvid pilgrimage. I have gone from myth times to the world of today, from the world of magic to the world of science, in the name of Raven. As part of my research, I met with people from the Raven Clan (a leadership clan) of the Kwakiutl and Haida peoples, I discussed shamanic healing with Raven priests, I reviewed the writings of tribal historians describing the lives of great leaders guided by ravens and crows, and I met with scientists who love and understand ravens and crows not for their magical powers but for the beautiful and intelligent birds they are.

In any project of this sort, there are certain people whose assistance proves invaluable. I was fortunate in my research and travels, because admirers and students of these birds freely shared their thoughts, expertise, and in many cases, their homes with me.

During my travels on Vancouver Island, I met many remarkable people. Among the tribes of the Great Northwest, stories and dances are clan and personal property. To share a story with a person, to "give" a person a story, is to give that person a special gift; it also shows them honor. In potlatch societies, there is nothing nobler or more prestigious than giving, and I appreciate the gifts that these people gave me. George Taylor, a Kwakiutl Raven-dancer, explained to me that "Raven is everything. He is spiritual strength, he is power, he is the past, and he is the future. He is the essence of my people."

In a Catholic cathedral in Victoria, there is a beautifully carved collection of Salishan boxes, each depicting in traditional art forms Christian New Testament stories. In older days, these large cedar boxes held food for the living and served as caskets for the dead. These particular boxes serve as the church's main altar. On the most beautiful box, there is a painted carving called "Raven-Woman: Mary Pregnant with the Word." It shows a Salishan woman, wrapped in the wings of White Raven, travelling to Vancouver Island in a cedar canoe beneath a shining sun, accompanied by dolphin messengers. The Salishan creator of this beautiful box is Charles Elliott.

Struck by the mastery of the piece, in which I saw Raven the Transformer, I located Elliott and requested an interview. He invited me to his home on the Salish reserve. We met, and I was treated to an afternoon with the artist and his family. He said that what I perceived was correct, what he had carved *was* Raven transforming; what the Church chose to see was her own interpretation. Elliott gave me a great gift that day, two Raven stories. One was a serious story about Raven and people after the Great Flood, the second was about Raven and his sisters, the Crows, picking berries (the latter is included in this book).

Two others from this island must be thanked. The first is anthropologist Kevin Neary of the Royal British Columbia Provincial Museum, who kindly guided me through various exhibits and put me in contact with Raven George Taylor and Charles Elliott. The second is mathematician Owen Brandon, who became a friend and has supported my work through his own research and an assortment of newsclippings, articles, and rare books about ravenlore and Canadian Indian affairs.

I also want to thank Russell Barsh, an attorney and lecturer at the University of Washington Law School, for his interviews and assistance. Barsh and I were introduced through contacts at the United Nations, where he does important human rights work through that organization and his legal advocacy.

I would not have learned the details of the prophecies of Circling Raven had it not been for the interest of Spokane attorney Robert Dellwo. Mr. Dellwo is one of the most outstanding Indian law attorneys in North America; I didn't know this when I attended high school at Holy Names Academy with his daughter Madeline. I learned about Mr. Dellwo's remarkable contributions to the corpus of Indian law during research at Spokane's Museum of Native American Cultures.

I want to thank the staff of that museum, not only for bringing me to Spokane in 1989 to lecture about Indian affairs and the Navajo and Hopi land dispute, but for their support of my raven research in the autumn of 1990 as well. Special thanks are due museum staffer Jan Wigen, who initially invited me to Spokane. Museum archivist and photo collection curator Kaye Hale deserves a special note of thanks, because she encouraged my interest in Crow and the Ghost Dance, and through her encouragement, new worlds of research were opened. Museum director Lynette Miller, an expert in Pacific Coastal art, deserves thanks for her support as well.

I also want to thank Raymond Reyes of the Gonzaga University Indian Studies project. Raymond's enthusiasm and appreciation of the Raven people was contagious and he helped me tremendously. Through him, I met Bobby Lake, the shaman Medicine Grizzly Bear. Lake freely shared his knowledge (with the encouragement of the Bird People), and I cannot thank him enough for his unselfish gift of time.

Special thanks go to Dr. Curtis Hinsley, former chairman of the History Department at Northern Arizona University; his support of my research and academic endeavors and his encouragement of my teaching were greatly appreciated. Thanks are also due Dr. Loline Hathaway and the staff of the Navajo Nation Zoological and Botanical Park for their continued interest in my work.

It is said by some people that the world of science and the world of nature and philosophy must forever remain separated. Those who maintain this have never met Dr. Lawrence Kilham. All people interested in birds owe a great debt to Dr. Kilham and his wife Jane. I read interviews with Dr. Kilham in a national magazine and knew I had to read his book, *The American Crow and Common Raven.* Physician, historian, naturalist, and educator, Dr. Kilham is one of the greatest men I've ever met. His willingness to correspond with me, his kindness in meeting with me, and the graciousness he and his family showed me in New Hampshire were most appreciated. Though I am not a naturalist, and have only started to explore the intricacies of raven and crow behavior, the Kilhams allowed me into their home and family circle and shared their time with me. I will always remember my climb up Holt's Ledge with Dr. Kilham's daughter Phoebe. Seeing the ravens at the summit made the exertion well worthwhile.

I also want to thank my brother Mike Feher for his hospitality during my weeks of research in Seattle and my father Ferenc X. Feher for his support of my work and his time during my research in Spokane.

Finally, I want to thank my publisher and editor, Bruce Andresen and Susan McDonald, for suggesting this project. I have always loved ravens and crows, so the opportunity to write about them and their roles in North American societies was truly a blessing. Northland Publishing allowed me to walk among the raven people, and I appreciate their patience and support.

Ravensong Introductory Note
Penguin Edition

*R*aven, the Trickster, Magician and Creator, works in mysterious ways. I developed the idea for a series about totemic animals years ago, and *Ravensong* was the first book planned in that series. After the success of *Ravensong*, I made a decision to take another advanced degree and graduate school delayed fulfillment of my plan for a while. During the interim, however, I came to live with wolves in the mountains of Arizona and relocated for a professorship at a small college in Montana, heartland of the most successful wolf recovery in the United States. I fell in love with a beautiful wolf and his family, and realized *Wolfsong* would be a natural second book in the series. Raven the Transformer opened the way. I was able to find a publisher for a new version of *Ravensong* and the second in my totemic series, *Wolfsong*.

Ravensong and the *Naturesong* books live thanks to the hard work of many people. First and foremost, I want to thank my editor, Sara Carder, for her interest in and support of my work. I thank my agent, Jenny Bent, for her love of the mystical, magical, and mysterious, and her reading of my work. I thank

Larry Ormsby and Carole Thickstun, artists from the first edition of *Ravensong* and our forthcoming wolf book. But most of all, I want to express my appreciation and love for Raven and all the creatures who make up the complicated web of life. I love living in a place where I can watch eagles feed their young high atop cliff eyries. I love living in a place where I can watch young buffalo calves romp in the spring sunlight and hear wolves howling to the full moon beneath indigo skies. I write about what I love, and I love Nature. Many thanks to those who enable me to continue writing about those I love.

Catherine Feher-Elston
Lame Deer, Montana
Summer 2004

Introduction

avens and crows *(Corvidae)* are special birds. From the dawn of human memory, they have been associated with healing, magic, and successful hunting. Shamanic birds, honored by almost all human societies, many things about them remain mysterious despite their long association with people. In recent years, scientists have made major breakthroughs in understanding corvid societies and behavior, but much remains to be learned and understood.

This book focuses on two members of the corvid family and their role in North American societies. Raven and crow speak to us in many voices: in myth and dreams, in songs and chants of religious ritual, in diagrams and statistics of science. Ravensong is more than the call of birds; it is a philosophy, a process. It is a history of human thought and experience.

Most American children of the 1950s remember the television cartoon crows Heckle and Jeckle, a mischievous duo who schemed to con people into giving them food and money. Not all Americans view crows with benevolence, however, especially farmers who have to deal with their depredations.

American raven and crow populations are flourishing, in part because of the increase in edible material discarded by humans, but also because they are one of the most adaptable and successful avian species on earth.

There was a time when ravens and crows were held sacred by almost all native peoples of the Americas. Colonial-era chronicler Roger Williams, writing about the New England tribes in 1643, recorded the reverence of these people for crows. The Algonquins told him that while crows did sometimes damage their corn, they would not hurt or kill crows because their elders taught them that crows had brought human beings gifts of seed corn and beans from the field of the Great Creator God Cautantouwit. This god and his crow emissaries lived in a happy spirit world with other gods and the spirits of good people. The souls of evildoers were not allowed to enter the fields of the great god, but were doomed to wander eternally without rest.

Ravens and crows were almost always considered to be messengers between the living and the spirit worlds. They were associated with life and growing things as well as with the great beyond. The birds were also appreciated for their comic abilities, their incredible range of vocalization, and their intelligence.

Nearly all tribes have stories featuring a mischievous animal-god whose curiosity and desire to exploit others inevitably gets the trickster into trouble. Raven is the epitome of the Divine Trickster in Beringia and the Pacific Northwest. He shares this role with Coyote in the Rocky Mountains and

among the peoples
of the Plains and the
Southwest, and with
Rabbit in the Southeast.
Raven is a dual character:
he can be selfish, greedy,
and lazy as well as noble of
character; this nobility manifests itself in compassion, gregari-
ousness, and wisdom. Despite his
propensity for making trouble, compassionate Raven is always willing to come to the
assistance of the persecuted and weak.

Many European societies once honored the Raven, the
Earth Mother, and all of the natural powers those entities

represented. Ravens and crows were believed to be omniscient, to know all things past, present, and to come. Celtic Europeans associated these birds with many forms of the Earth Mother. Raven has long been the symbol of leadership as well as magic. It is said that Odin, father of the Norse and Teutonic gods, was accompanied in his travels by two ravens, Thought and Memory; he sent them out to survey the world each morning, and instructed them to bring back all the news to him. In Finland and other Baltic countries, ravens and crows are still affiliated with wisdom and medicine. Raven was the totem of the Hunnish and Magyar leaders, and a great Hungarian king bore the raven as part of his family coat-of-arms.

The Pacific Northwest, a land where mountains rise up from the sea, becoming islands sparkling like diamonds beneath a golden sun, is the stronghold of Raven religion. Anthropologists say that Asiatic peoples, following game from Siberia across Beringia, brought Raven religion and shamanism with them when they entered Alaska and dispersed throughout the New World. Raven's children—the Haida, the Kwakiutl, the Koyukon, the Tlingit—and many other tribal groups find these anthropological anecdotes amusing, but they know that Raven did not "come" from anywhere— he always was, and always will be. In Raven's world, gods and humans meet in ways contemporary Europeans are only beginning to comprehend. Raven is eternal, Raven religion is eternal, and Raven lives.

MYTH TIME

Carex's World

A sonorous voice calls out, soothing, melodious, beckoning across the treetops of the deep forest. Raven extends an invitation to enter his realm—an ancient world of beauty and myth, magic and power. Raven's world is inhabited by many beings. In his world, all things—animals, plants, rocks, trees—have spirits. To enter Raven's world is to enter a place where human beings are newcomers. Divine Raven and his descendants seen today across the tundras, mountains, deserts, and forests of North America come from a time long before man.

Raven's play encompasses both the creative and destructive forces of life. It is said that when Raven created the first world, he made everything perfect, a world full of happiness and beauty, without pain, suffering, or ugliness. But Raven grew bored with this perfect world and started reshaping things. Although he loved beauty, he created imperfections and new creatures with faults and foibles so he could entertain himself with them. Man was one of the many imperfect beings Raven brought into this world.

Raven loves mankind because he put much of himself into human nature when he made people. He enjoys human company, he laughs at human greed, gluttony, and silliness, because he sees his own faults in them. He also admires human courage and perseverance. Raven finds the human propensity for violence and wholesale slaughter distasteful, however. He was distraught when he saw the First People killing many of his creations, but then thought that, since wolves eat caribou and caribou eat grass, perhaps it was the nature of humans to kill. Divine Raven will never die, so he knows little about fear. He has been known to assume mortal form in order to experience human emotions. Because of such transformations, Raven has learned respect for humans, their determination, their ability to overcome fear, and their adaptability.

From the time of their first contact with Raven, humans have both loved and feared his power. They laugh at his comic antics, admire his strength and gregarious nature. Shaman priests enlist his aid in making people well, and hunters pray for his blessings to feed their families. Humans still tell stories about Great Raven, still make prayers to him, still honor him and his children. After all, while there is only one Great Raven, one never knows when he may take the form of the mundane raven or crow.

Early humans revered Great Raven, and today, people from Beringia into Canada and throughout North America honor him as well. One of the earliest cave paintings at Lascaux details the life story of a Raven priest. Many Paleolithic paintings and stone inscriptions chronicle the lives of Raven shamans,

their births, their ceremonies, their victories, deaths, and
ultimate transformation after death from human to raven form.
They knew that, despite their human faults and weaknesses,
he would not forsake them. He answered their prayers and
helped them in their times of need.

As time went by, however, some forgot his divine role;
they turned away from Raven and the great Earth religions.
They lost many things. These people developed diverse cultures and civilizations throughout Europe, the Levant, and
North Africa. Ultimately, as though closing a vast circle, they
came into contact with humans who had not forgotten their
origins and their relationship with Raven and Earth Mother.
For five centuries, fierce war raged between the invaders who
had forgotten and the people who had remembered.

Today, most of the wars over land between these groups
have ended, and Europeans and others who followed from
the Old World to the New are beginning to realize that they
can no longer separate themselves from the Earth and their
fellow creatures. Scientists are rediscovering and relearning
things that Raven's children have always known; they are
finally recognizing the logic and wisdom of the natural order.

To understand Raven's world, one must return to the
world of myth. To some, this requires a suspension of reality.
When one enters Raven's world, myth, philosophy, and
science intertwine. Westerners may believe that they alone are
the masters of the universe, that only they hold the keys to
knowledge. Such people walk alone in the World of Man all
the days of their lives, never realizing that Raven's world is all

around them. There are those, however, who answer Raven's call and accept his invitations. They reach out their hands and open their eyes, and the invisible veil between the world of people and the world of Raven is lifted.

Why Raven
Is Black and the
World Imperfect

In the long ago, when the world was young, in the time before Man, Raven was white as snow. White Raven's soul was filled with light and beauty, and his spirit shone like the sun. His twin brother was also beautiful to behold, but although he was shiny, his soul, like his feathers, was dark and black as deepest night.

Raven, Shaper of Mountains, loved to make new things. In his efforts to make the perfect animal, he created many beings, ancestors of life in the world today. White Raven was a creator, a lover of life, and when he laughed in happiness at seeing what he had made, the sun broke through the cloud, making rainbows dance across the sky and warming the earth.

White-feathered Raven delighted in beauty, and he breathed joy and happiness into everything he made. But his brother, the Dark One, was brooding and miserable. He also created things, but his creations were ugly and nasty—leeches, ticks, and monsters—things reflecting his own mean spirit. He delighted in destroying, damaging, and undoing White Raven's creations. The blackness in the Dark One's heart extended to every aspect of his being.

One day, as White Raven, deep in concentration, carefully painted the delicate colors on Puffin, his brother stealthily crept up to the paint box. Dark One dumped the paint box on the ground, smearing the colors and smashing the cedar box.

"Stop it! Stop it!" White Raven shouted. "Why do you do this?" The Dark One only laughed at his brother's anger. Later, when White Raven thought about the incident, he concluded that his brother was in a bad mood, and didn't worry too much about his misbehavior, as he was preoccupied with his quest to make the perfect animal.

In his mind's eye, White Raven envisioned a poised and delicate creature, with four graceful and beautiful legs, with four jet-black shiny pointed hoofs that went click-click-tap-tap when it walked. The creature would be fleet-footed, and run with the wind. It would be russet-red in color, with huge, soft, brown eyes, moist with love and compassion. It would be a friend to all, and serve as a counselor to the world. For its crowning beauty, White Raven would make a lattice of beautiful antlers. Raven sat down and began shaping his vision into reality.

He had just finished his work and was bending down breathing life into the first deer when Dark One crept up behind him. Just as Raven was giving instructions to Deer about how to behave, Dark One jumped out and yelled at Deer, terrifying him and causing him to run away. (Deer has been timid and skittish ever since, and unable to be the even-tempered counselor Raven had envisioned.) Raven scowled at his brother.

"Why do you do this?" he asked. Raven was dismayed at the interference of the Dark One, but his kindness and his desire for creating beauty overcame his irritation and like a cloud passing across the face of the sun, the dismay was quickly forgotten. Raven returned to the work of building the world.

One day, after much labor, Raven was putting the finishing touches on a beautiful fish. The fish had sinuous curves and was designed for strength and strong swimming. *Ah, this fish is truly perfect,* Raven thought. *What colors shall I paint it?* he asked himself as he considered the beautifully arched back. Suddenly, from his hiding place in the woods near the shoreline, Dark One rushed out and stepped on the fish, crushing its arch and changing its graceful form to squatty flatness. It became the first flounder.

"Why do you do this?" Raven cried out. "You want everything to be ugly, you hate what is beautiful in the world, and you are only happy when you hurt or destroy. If you damage another of my creatures, I shall surely kill you!"

Dark One laughed and tormented his brother. "Only one thing can kill me, the same thing that can kill you: an axe," he said.

"An axe? Well, maybe that will kill you, but only a whip can kill me," Raven said. Raven was lying to his brother because he had become suspicious of him after all of the cruelty he had observed. He feared his brother might try to kill him.

That night, when the moon was full and the earth was bathed in the cool beauty of its beams, Dark One crept up to his brother as he slept, and the loud crack of a whip echoed through the stillness of the night.

"Ouch! Ouch! Ouch!" Raven cried, rising from his bed in pain and anger. "Is there no limit to your evil?" Raven screamed at his brother, grabbing an axe. In anger, Raven drove the axe deep into his brother's skull. Blood spewed from the splintered skull, splattering Raven's white feathers and covering him with gore.

As he watched his brother die, all anger left Raven and his heart filled with remorse. Raven, lover of life, was horrified at his actions. He looked down at his mountain-maker hands in disgust and shame. He, who had until now only created life, had brought death to his own brother.

As the blood stained his feathers, a darkness gripped his heart and his soul. Try as he might to wash out the blood of his murdered brother, the dark stain spread, covering his body. He felt a transformation inside himself, too. It was as if the soul of his lost twin had entered into him and where joy and the love of life had once been, a darkness and a brooding prevailed. Raven was overcome with sadness, and he withdrew from the world in deep grief.

"What will become of me, how can I create now that I have destroyed?" Raven moaned in his sorrow. "And what

about my quest for making the most perfect creature of all—
a two-legged creature, with an intellect as bright and reflective
as my own, wise and compassionate, filled with love and
wonder of all that I have made? I was going to call this creature a Human Being. But I feel a darkness, a coldness in my
heart; my twin has become one with me, and I fear I will
never be able to make perfection."

Wretched Raven wandered in the deep forests of the
North Country, overcome with remorse. As time passed, he
regained his love of life and determined to resume his making
of the world. He returned to his plan of creating Human
Beings. But Raven's appearance had changed forever. His
body, once covered with bright, white feathers, brilliant as the
sun, was now clothed in feathers of deepest black, shining,
shimmering mirrors of jet and the dazzling sheen of diamonds,
reflecting both the daylight and the moonlight. Raven's nature
had transformed, too. Where once there had only been compassion, love, and joy, now also were cunning, mischief, and
greediness. Most of the time, the old Raven's goodness overcame the darkness of his brother's spirit, but sometimes the bad
would overcome the good, and Raven would do foolish and
wicked things, things he later regretted.

Raven made many Human Beings, but none turned out
exactly as he envisioned. Some were too tall, some were too
short, some had beautiful forms but bad tempers. Some were
beautiful in their spirit, but ugly or misshapen in their form.
Some were clever, like Raven, but also greedy and self-seeking.
Others had wisdom and compassion and were beautiful to
see, but too often their fellow Human Beings would not

listen to their knowledge and learn from the wisdom Raven offered through his creations.

"Hmm," Raven said aloud. "Maybe it isn't just me. Maybe this is the way of things—maybe Human Beings are meant to be a combination of all things—good and evil, beautiful and ugly, wise and silly. Maybe I should accept this and leave things this way. After all, I myself am now a combination of good and evil, since my brother and I now share one soul in my black body. Maybe this is the nature of things."

So Raven gave up on perfecting Human Beings, and molded other creatures. He created all the creatures of the world, and as a result, all creatures have duality, a good and a bad side. The bear, while strong and big, is lazy and always hungry. The beaver, while hard-working and industrious, must chew down trees, the homes of the Bird People, in order to build his own cozy lodge. The skunk, while lovely with his heavy fur coat and beautiful black-and-white markings, emits a terrible stench when frightened. And Raven's direct descendants, clever and beautiful birds, while clever and wily, are afraid and skittish in new situations. They are also gluttons.

Because of the evil nature of Raven's twin, and Raven's righteous anger and subsequent murder of his brother, Raven is black and the world imperfect, despite all his efforts and his abiding love for life and all his creatures. Still, on days of bright sunlight, when Raven flies against the sky, Raven the Transformer sometimes reassumes his brilliant white plumage and dazzles the world with his beauty.

Raven
Frees the
Light

Northwest Coast

Long ago, long ago, darkness covered the earth. Raven, Creator of the World, stumbled in the darkness and stubbed his toe. "That's enough of all this fumbling around in blackness. I must do something about it," Raven muttered in his pain.

Raven examined his bruised toe as well as he could, and, as it was cold, fluffed his feathers and hunkered down, carefully placing warm, soft feathers over the injured digit. As he crouched on the hard ground, Raven thought to himself, and remembered the beautiful daughter of an ugly and selfish old man.

He had heard stories about this old man, about how he had a collection of boxes, each one nestled inside of the other. Inside one of these boxes was the relief to the suffering of darkness.

Raven remembered that this beautiful girl had long and flowing hair, hair as glossy and lustrous as the Raven's wing, and lived in a cedar house beside a river. Raven wanted to learn more about the girl, and was extremely curious about the rumors. Raven pulled his injured foot up closer to his body and balanced on one leg. After dozing and warming his foot, he stretched his wings and flew up into the sky, heading north toward the cedar house.

As Raven approached the cedar house, he heard the thin voice of the old man singing about his treasures. The man sang of cedar boxes nestled within cedar boxes, and the wonderful treasures secreted within the smallest box. Hearing the singing, Raven knew that he had found the right place. An accomplished thief, Raven thought that it would be easy to steal the box of light. The challenge would be getting access to the house.

Raven's mind turned and turned as he perched high in the branches of a hemlock tree outside of the cedar house. As Raven roosted, plotting, the old man's daughter came out of the house carrying a basket for water. Raven scrutinized her form, and his sharp ears registered her footsteps. As she walked to the stream, Raven flapped his wings and flew through the trees; the darkness hid him from the girl.

Raven the Transformer had devised a scheme to get into the cedar house. He flew upstream from the innocent maiden, changed himself into a hemlock needle, and fell into the stream. As the girl dipped her basket into the cool, running water, Raven was caught. The girl took a strong, deep drink, and Raven slid down her throat and into her belly. Raven then found a soft place, deep in the girl's womb, and transformed himself into a fetus.

All of this transformation made Raven sleepy, and he curled up for a long nap. He slept for several months and his fetus-form grew and developed into a healthy boy-child. He was normal in all ways, except that he had a beak-like protuberance covered with skin for his nose. Finally, he came forth from the girl in the same way as human children. Naturally, the girl loved the little Raven-baby, although in the darkness she could not see him well. The old man, Raven-baby's grandfather, loved his daughter, and naturally, doted on his grandson, too.

It was indeed greedy and selfish of the old man to hoard the world's light, but he truly loved Raven-baby, and sang songs to him and cuddled him and made all kinds of toys for him. Of course, Raven was mindful of his mission, the freeing of the light and, with his bright and shiny raven-eyes, was constantly peering around the cedar house, looking for those boxes within boxes.

A huge carved cedar box stood in one corner of the house. After much study, Raven was convinced that this must be the box containing all the other boxes, and the light. Raven-boy toddled over to the box. Despite his human form, he still had a slight waddle when he walked, the same waddle ravens have when they walk on the ground in the deep woods in the heat of the day. Raven looked around to be sure that he was alone— the girl and her father had walked down to the stream together. But just as Raven lifted the lid of the big box, the old man walked in and scolded Raven-boy for touching his most prized possession. He told him never to touch that box again, thus confirming Raven's suspicion that he had indeed found the right box.

From that day on, Raven-boy constantly cajoled his grandfather to give him the big, carved cedar box. When the old man said no, Raven-boy howled and cried and begged some more. Finally, the old man, out of love for the child, relented, and taking other, smaller boxes from inside, gave him the outer box. Raven-boy continued to cajole and one by one, he accumulated the other boxes.

Finally, Raven had been given all of the boxes except the smallest one containing the light. A glow emanated from this box, and Raven-boy demanded it, too, as a gift from his grandfather.

"Absolutely not," Grandfather said. Raven-boy started crying. He howled and yowled.

"Give it to me, give it to me. I want the box. I want to see inside," he squawked.

Finally, the old man relented. He opened the box and tossed it to Raven-boy. In an instant, Raven transformed into his old self, swooped down upon the light, and taking it in his beak, flew up the

smokehole and out into the open sky. Raven the Transformer
lit up the world.

Looking back over his shoulder, he saw the girl, his mother,
in sunlight for the first time. She was indeed very beautiful.
As Raven flew carrying the light in his beak, he saw the world
that he had created. He saw the stark and rugged mountains,
he saw the trees, he saw boulders and rivers and the villages of
men, with their carved cedar poles chronicling the history of
the clans. Raven enjoyed the beauty of his creation.

*Cedar box from
Northwest coast,
1850s*

Suddenly, he felt a shadow and saw the talons of a big eagle close to him. Startled, Raven opened his beak and dropped the light. It hit the earth and broke into three pieces. Two pieces bounced up into the air and became the moon and the stars. Raven retrieved the third piece, and carrying it in his beak, flew beyond the boundaries of earth and sky and pushed the light out, far away from the earth.

Raven put the sun in its proper place, and there it warms us, gives us light, and sustains life even to this day.

Raven and
the Ancestral
Human Beings

Haida, British Columbia

Everyone knows that a long time ago, the world was covered by a gigantic flood. It covered up islands, shores, and even many of the mountains. Eventually, the flood receded. Raven was flying around, happy that the floodwaters were gone. He was bored with a waterlogged world. So he was out there, flying around, flying around. Finally, hungry Raven landed on a beach and began looking for good things to eat.

Raven hopped and flapped along the seashore. His feet left tracks in the sand, and the sea rushed in and washed them away. From a distance, as Raven hopped along the beach, he spied a gigantic clamshell. Always interested in anything new or different, Raven waddled over to the shell. He heard strange sounds coming from that clamshell—little squeaks and funny noises: "Yakity, yak-yak." He had never heard such sounds coming from a clamshell before. He cocked his head and fixed his shiny black eye on the shell.

Raven pecked at the shell with his sharp beak. For a moment, the squeaks stopped and the shell was quiet, although the rush of the wind and the pounding of the surf continued. Raven backed away from the shell, and within a short time, the squeaks and shrieks started again. Raven's curiosity got the better of him, and again he waddled up to the shell. "Hmm," Raven said aloud. "What could be in there—maybe something good to eat?" (Gluttonous Raven is always hungry, regardless of how recently he has eaten.)

This clamshell was really big. Raven's shadow crossed over the shell, and once again, the squeaks stopped. Raven realized that whatever was in that clamshell was afraid of his shadow. He was curious to find out what was inside the shell, but he knew that he would have to soothe its fears, whatever it was.

Raven has a beautiful voice; he can croon and sound like a beautiful bell. He can sing and make pleasant and reassuring sounds, comforting sounds, sounds that bring joy to any heart. So Raven decided to sing to the clamshell. He sang a song that sounded like gurgling and happy water. After his song, he called out to the shell, "Come out, whatever you are, whoever you are. Come out. I am Raven, Creator of the World, and I will not hurt you. Please come out and play with me.

The flood is over, I have given light to the world. Please come out and we will play together."

Again Raven sang. Raven is not only the Maker of Things, not only the Transformer, he is also a Magician and a Healer. His singing contains magic and his voice, while sometimes annoying when he is hungry or frightening when he is angry, can also be lulling and soothing. Finally, the clamshell opened, and a little being with long black hair, a round head, and brown, smooth skin popped out. Raven looked at this creature, with two legs like himself (but no feathers) and two arms and two hands: a very puny and scrawny being. Raven heard the murmur of other voices in the shell. Because he didn't want to scare the little thing, he continued singing, and he called the others out. Slowly, these little creatures emerged from the clamshell and onto the beach of what is today called British Columbia. These beings were the ancestral Haida.

"Come and play in my beautiful world, a world with warm, rich sunshine and sounding seas and dark nights for telling stories and sleeping. Come and play with me, and we will eat salmon and berries and all types of good things," Raven sang to the First People.

At first, the People were frightened and bewildered. They were frightened of the sea-noise, the crashing of waves against rocks, and the pounding of the surf. They were frightened by the sound and movement of the wind. They were frightened by the darkness and size of Raven; they were afraid Raven might eat them. But slowly, one by one, they emerged and played with Raven and ate the delicacies he brought to share with them. (Sharing food was a most generous gesture for Raven, who usually prefers others to feed him, and is always scheming to get delicious meals with little effort.)

Raven played with the First People for a long time; he taught them many things. He was amazed at how clever and courageous they were. Finally, Raven realized that all of these creatures were male, so by his magic, he created females and he taught the people how to have children. Finally, Raven grew tired of playing with the ancestral Haida on the beach. He flew away to take care of other things, but he still came to visit the Haida every now and then.

After their emergence from the clamshell with the encouragement of Raven, the Haida became a mighty people. They developed fine villages and carvings that told stories of their emergence and the history of their clans and families. Raven taught them to cure sickness with herbs and songs and magic. They made prayers to the Raven, and continue to do so to this day. They know that Raven is the Creator of the World, they know that the world goes through many cycles. They know that the time of Human Beings may not last forever but that Raven the Transformer, Raven, Bringer of Light, is one who is, was, and always will be.

Crow
Doctors
Raven

Tse-Shaht of Canada

Everybody knows what a glutton Raven is. Once, on a day in the long ago, Raven's greediness got him into serious trouble and it was only through the compassion of Crow that his pain was eased.

In the long ago, Raven, Crow, Squirrel, and other animals and spirits lived among men. Yes, you say, they still live among men. And this is true, but long ago, the animal-spirits lived in villages alongside men, in their own houses, and they spoke in the language of humans. This was long ago, when creation had only just been completed.

Raven was always hungry. His shiny black eyes were constantly on the lookout for something good to eat, and his stomach was always rumbling in anticipation of that something good. The first little boy deer lived in the same village as the greedy raven, and the bird watched the fawn playing, scampering and jumping and squealing with delight throughout the village and the land and forests around it. The little deer was plump and looked very juicy and appetizing to Raven. Raven watched the deer romp with his village playmates, and smiled as he thought secret thoughts and schemed about ways to lure the happy little deer into the woods, where he would gobble him up.

"Oh pretty long-eared little deer, come with me, and we will play together in the forest," Raven invited the fawn. "We will have so much fun. Let's go."

"Oh, I wish I could go into the forest with you, beautiful Raven, but my mother forbids me to go into the woods without her. And I always obey my mother," Son of Deer replied.

"Well, I certainly wouldn't want you to disobey your mother," Raven said. But Raven's hunger for the deer would not be ignored. He thought devious thoughts, mumbling to himself, concentrating his efforts on forming his evil plan. People heard him muttering as he wandered around the village, but it was low and hard to understand.

One day, when the little deer was on the shoreline near the village canoes, Raven flew up and croaked, "Come with me into the woods. I have learned a new game, and I want to teach it to you."

The little deer loved games, and his soft eyes grew wide at Raven's words. But he remembered his mother's orders, and told Raven, "Well, I know lots of games. So what." But in his heart, he really wanted to learn what Raven had offered.

Raven cocked his head and slowly looked around to see if anyone else was on the beach. "No one knows this game but me. And since you are my very best friend, I wanted to share it with you. Then you and I can play, and it will be our game, our very own secret game. No one else will know. It will be our secret," wicked Raven coaxed. "Let's go up into the cliffs overlooking the village. I can teach you there, and you will still be within the view of the village, not in the woods at all."

The little deer, overcome with curiosity but fearful of getting caught and still not quite sure of Raven's motives, reluctantly held back from agreeing to go. "But my mother says…"

Raven was impatient. He leaned over and whispered into the long, soft ears of the fawn, "Oh, come on. It's not in the woods; I'll be with you, don't worry. We're best friends, remember?"

The deer shook himself and looked around to see if anyone was watching. "Well," he said hesitantly, "well, let's go, but only long enough to learn the game, and then I must go home."

Raven's mouth watered as he hopped up the hill to the cliffs overlooking the village, anticipating his feast. The deer's little hooves went clack-clack-clack as he scampered up the rocky hill. Once on top, he felt better—he wasn't in the forest, and he wasn't *really* disobeying his mother. "Show me the new game," he said, as he stamped his hooves impatiently.

Raven leaned over and with a gleam in his eye, said, "It is a new game—a game never played before. It is called the crying game."

The little deer stared at Raven, and then he said, "Crying? Why should I want to cry? I am so happy, I don't like crying. I am not sad. Why should I cry? It doesn't sound like a fun game to me. I'm going home." Son of Deer started backing away from Raven.

"Oh, come on. It is really fun. Think about your old grandparents, that once were and are no more. Doesn't that make you sad?" wily, wicked Raven said. "Think about your old grandparents. Watch me—watch what I do. Awahooo-booo-hoooo-owwww. . .oooo, my poor old grandparents that once were and are no more. Lean way, way back, tilt your head back." Raven's face was the image of sorrow, and he cried real tears in his attempt to impress the little boy deer.

"I don't think I had any grandparents," the fawn said, backing away, closer to the edge of the cliff. But the gentle heart of the little creature had been touched by Raven's tears and he felt tears welling up in his own eyes.

"Give it a try," Raven said, as he hopped closer to the precipice. He edged even closer, and called to the little deer. "Come over here, sit beside me. Come and play my new game. I think you will really enjoy it once you give it a try."

The big-eyed deer walked over and sat in front of Raven. Raven turned him around so that his back was toward the cliff's edge, and gave him a little nudge closer to the edge. Then he spun him. "Now, bend your head way, way back, stretch your neck, and pretend to cry. Be sure to close your eyes," Raven encouraged.

The little deer leaned his head and shoulders backward, oblivious to the danger. Remembering the look of despair on Raven's face, the little deer cried real tears. "Oh-oh-oh, my poor old grandparents that were," the deer cried. Wicked Raven seized his opportunity. He pushed the poor little deer right over the edge of the cliff.

Son of Deer fell, and Raven flapped his wings and descended with him. Before the little deer hit the ground, Raven gobbled him up in one big gulp. "Yum," said Raven, smacking his lips as he landed at the base of the cliffs. His stomach was finally full; for once in his life, Raven was not hungry. In fact, his stomach was so full, it was actually bulging. When Raven tried to fly, the weight of the little deer prevented lift-off. Raven started feeling sleepy and as the sun was getting low, he decided to go home. He waddled into his house in the village and collapsed in exhaustion.

Deep in the stupor of gluttony, Raven dreamed. He dreamed of the comfort of a full stomach, and then he dreamed that there was tremendous pressure in his stomach, a sharp, pointy pressure. Suddenly, Raven awoke from his troubled sleep.

Raven felt sick. His stomach really hurt. "Oh-ow-ow. . . Oh-ow-ow," Raven moaned. "Oh, I am sick. I feel soooo-sooo sick." Raven's moans grew louder and louder as his stomach began to expand. Neighbors heard him and worried. A kind person sent for the village doctor—a little female crow.

The crow-doctor hopped to Raven's front door and peered

in. "Oh Raven, what have you done?" she cried. She sang a medicine song, but she did not go inside Raven's house. Crow knew what caused Raven's pain; she could see the past, present, and future. She sang her medicine song, and as she sang, some village people commented that Son of Deer had not come home, although it was long after dark, and his mother was worried.

Raven, wrapped in his sleeping robes, moaned and groaned. "Oh, Crow, help me, help me, I think I am dying," oversated Raven begged.

Some men went into Raven's house, and carried him outside. Raven clung to his sleeping robe, holding it tight over his belly.

"Help me, Crow," Raven begged. "It hurts so much."

"I guess that's what you get for being greedy," Crow said. "Let me take a look." She snatched the blanket away from Raven, and the assembled villagers gasped at what they saw. Protruding from Raven's distended belly was the shape of two young-deer antlers.

The men carried Raven away and sliced his belly open, and out stepped Son of Deer, shaken but whole; greedy Raven had swallowed him in one big gulp. "Mother, Mother, I will never disobey you again," the little deer cried, and ran away home to his mother's side.

Raven was left bleeding and alone, but his stomach was greatly relieved to be rid of its burden. Patient Crow flew to Raven's side, stitched up his belly, and gave him soothing herbs to help him sleep and heal. She made no judgmental remarks—she just took care of him.

Raven
Gets Caught
in a Lie

Lower Coast Salish of Vancouver Island

One day in the early fall, when the salmon were running and the skies were bright and clear, allowing the sun to warm the earth, Raven and his little sisters, the crows, decided to go out and pick blackberries.

The rolling hills of southern Vancouver Island were thick with blackberry bushes, and the beautiful berries were ripening under the sun's warm benediction. Raven told his sisters that he knew just the place to find the ripest, most succulent berries in the hills behind a beach, a short canoe-trip away from their home village. So the little crows, happy at the prospect of a blackberry feast, eagerly gathered their food baskets and together with Raven, hopped into a big canoe.

Raven started out paddling the short distance to the black-berry cove, but after a few minutes, announced that he was exhausted, too tired to paddle further. "After all," Raven told his sisters, "It is such a warm and sunny day. I am so sleepy. You take over and let me doze here in the canoe and I'll help you gather the berries from the hills when we get there." So the crows took over the work of paddling, and Raven sprawl-ed out in the back of the cedar canoe and snoozed.

Raven awoke with a start when the dugout landed on the beach. "What, we're here already?" Raven mumbled. "I am so tired. Well, the bushes are right over there, you can't miss them, they're everywhere." Lazy Raven pointed towards the plain at the foot of the forested hills. Heavily laden black-berry bushes, with their sweet, plump, juicy berries, lined the beach and extended through the forest thickets and up the hillsides as far as the eye could see.

"Here, I'll help you unload these big baskets," Raven gal-lantly said to his sisters. "But I am still so sleepy; let me rest here in the canoe for a while and soon I will come up and help you gather."

The industrious crows strapped their burden-baskets across their foreheads and headed up the beach and into the woods. Raven promptly went to sleep, awakening only when the sisters brought basketloads of the delicious fruit to the boat, where they dumped them and immediately returned to the berry-brambles to collect more. As each basket was emptied,

Raven nibbled on the berries, eating one after another. Ravenous, gluttonous Raven gobbled each and every basketful of berries that his sisters brought to the canoe. As the shadows lengthened, Raven realized that he had eaten the crows' entire day's work. He knew that his sisters would be upset and angry when they returned and discovered his obnoxious behavior. Raven knew he was going to have to make up a story to explain the disappearance of the berries.

In those days, enemy raiders were everywhere, and they would overtake the unwary, looting and killing. Raven knew that he would have to make up a truly horrific tale, one that invoked his sisters' fear of raiders, in order to cover his greedy tracks. Plucking a few small tailfeathers, he threw them into the surf and muttered an enchantment to make the feathers look like enemy war canoes.

Raven's chest was crimson from the juice of the berries he had gobbled, so he ruffled up his feathers and plucked out a few from his breast, making himself look dishevelled and dam-

aged. He scattered the few remaining berries and the cedar
baskets and ran around making dozens of tracks to give the
appearance of a struggle. Then he collapsed on the sandy
beach beside the canoe. When he heard the happy cawing of
the crow sisters, he started moaning and wailing.

"Ow, ow, ow, ooooo. . ." Raven moaned. "What, am I still
in this world? Oh, my sisters, I am so glad that you are safe."
The crows crowded around Raven, concerned and worried.

"What happened? What happened?" they cried out in a
chorus.

"Enemy raiders, it was terrible. I tried to fight them off, as
you can see from the blood on my chest, but there were just
too many of them. They took all of our berries and paddled
away," Raven lied. "If you look out into the sea, you can see
their war canoes."

Raven pointed toward the enchanted feathers, and the
crows, out of love and concern, believed their brother. They
thought that they saw enemy canoes. "Oh, our poor brother,
we will bind your wounds and take you home," the worried
crows cried.

Covering his face with his hands, as if in pain, Raven
smiled a secret smile. His deception had worked. And indeed,
his stomach was starting to hurt as a result of stuffing so
many berries into it.

The crows loaded the canoes with their empty baskets;
they were saddened by the loss of a full day's labor but happy
that their brother was safe and alive. They had turned to lift
injured Raven into the canoe when a little snail called to them.

"Yoo-hoo, Crows, listen to me," little Snail called out to the homeward-bound group. "I have something to share with you. Some news to tell you."

Snail crawled up to the canoe, and pointed directly at Raven. "Shame, shame on you, naughty Raven, for deceiving your sisters," the indignant Snail said. "I saw it all, I tell you, and there was no enemy raid. Your lazy brother gobbled up all of your berries, and then told you a lie to hide his greediness."

The crows' concern turned to anger when they learned they had been deceived. "How could you do this to us, Raven?" they asked. "Is it really true, what he tells us?"

"I saw what you did, and I'm telling," little Snail told Raven accusingly. "You ate the berries, I saw what you did, naughty Raven."

"Ummmm. . .Well. . .look—you can see the canoes yourself; little Snail is lying, not me," Raven said weakly. He pointed toward the feathers in the sea, but the enchantment had worn off, and the crows saw the tailfeather pieces for what they really were. Upon closer examination of Raven, they realized that he was covered with berry juice, not blood. The crows mobbed Raven and boxed his ears, and for his punishment, made him row all the way back to the village to explain to everyone why there would be no blackberries for supper.

Raven,
the Shaman,
and the Lost Spirit

Beringia and Alaska

It was in the autumn of the year, long ago, on the day the first snowflakes gently fell, slowly curling down from the clouds onto the ground. It was the time after Raven had painted the leaves on the trees, and made the animals and the birds and molded Humans and given the gifts of healing, magic, music, and laughter to them. A man ran into the village where Raven lived, calling his name and asking where he could be found.

Raven was on the edge of the village, shaping hills with his mountain-maker's hands to protect some young fruit trees

from the cold blasts of the coming winter winds. He flew to
the man, who had come from very far away, and asked what
was wrong.

"Raven, we need your help," the man begged. "A great
evil has come into our village and we do not know what to do.
Some type of spirit has entered into our homes, and in spite
of the efforts of our best shamans, we cannot make contact
with it and find out what it needs. Instead, it takes food out
of the boiling cooking pots and throws it onto the ground,
where it gets dirty. Then, it throws it back into the pot, covered with dirt and leaves.

"Sometimes, the spirit becomes a strong wind, and tears
the roofs off of our houses. It mutters, 'Yes, no, Yes, no.'
Other times, it sweeps through our homes at night while we
sleep, tearing our sleeping robes to shreds and leaving us cold
and frightened," the man explained.

"One day when I was out fishing in my kayak, this spirit
knocked me right out of my boat, along with all of the fine
fish I had caught that day. I thought it was going to drown me
in the cold, cold sea, when suddenly, I found myself back in
the boat; all of my fish were also returned. Raven, we are
afraid because we do not know what this spirit is going to do
next, and we do not know what it wants or how to help it."
The man collapsed in tears. "Please come home with me, and
help us help the spirit, who must be in great distress to behave
in this strange way."

Raven sighed a deep sigh. He sat down on a stone and
thought to himself. *I really want to get on with my own work*

of building the world; there is so much to do. Winter is coming, and I want to protect my little trees. But I never ignore a prayer for help, and I love Human Beings, because they remind me so much of myself, and I did put a lot of myself into these brave creatures. Well, I have no choice, I must help them. Raven looked at the man.

"Stop crying. Tell me, what has the spirit said to the shamans?" Raven asked, and cocked his head to the side, his shiny eyes staring intensely at the man.

"The spirit always says the same thing, over and over and over. 'Yes-no-yes-no.' The words are always the same, but his actions are ever-changing." The man explained that the shamans used the strongest prayers and incantations in attempts to merge with the spirit, but in spite of their best efforts, the result was the same: "Yes-no-yes-no."

Raven nodded at the man. "This is very, very strange. Yes, I will help you; we will go back to your home village and wait for the next spirit-visit."

When Raven and his companion reached the village, all was in chaos. There were no roofs on the houses, water buckets were overturned, cooking fires were drenched, hunting spears and arrows broken, blankets shredded and wet. Children squalled and confused men and women shouted and ran around in circles as they tried to clean up the aftermath of what appeared to have been a terrific storm.

"It was here, as you can see," the man said to Raven. Raven peered around, looking at the chaos. He went from house to house, looking for something only he, a divine being, could see. Finally he stopped outside the head shaman's lodge.

"A-ha, there you are, sleeping, tired out after this big mess you made. What is wrong, how can I help you?"

The spirit uncurled itself, and started to cry, moaning and wailing in a most pathetic way. "Lost, lost, lost," the terrified spirit told Raven. "Lost, lost, lost, so scared."

Hearing the sadness and fear in the spirit-voice made Raven sad, and his eyes misted with tears for the poor lost one. "Calm down. I am Raven, Maker of the World, and I have come to help you. What can I do to make you happy, how can I help you?" Raven asked.

The spirit just cried, and as it cried, water flowed all around it and the shaman's house started to flood. "Calm yourself, and try to stop crying," Raven said. "What is it you want? A different form?"

"Yes-no-yes-no. I have had many forms. I recently left the body of a man. I have been many other things as well. I shared the body of a wolf, but I was hungry a lot of the time, so I shared the body of a deer, but I was frightened much of the time, and I didn't like that. I once transmigrated into the body of an eagle, but didn't like the heights and I was too lonely too much of the time. I just don't know what to do, or what I want to be now."

Raven sat down beside the spirit. "I can give you any form you want. What about a beautiful bird? You wouldn't have to fly too high, you could eat seeds and berries, and I could give you bright feathers. Would you like that?" Raven asked.

"Yes, I would like to be beautiful and eat seeds and berries, but no, what would it be like in the cold winter, maybe I would be hungry and maybe that would not be good. It might be good to be a bird, but then, it might not be good," the spirit said.

"Well, what about a beautiful black-and-white whale, who frolics in the sea and always has plenty to eat, who has no enemies, only friends. Would you like that?" Raven asked.

"Well, yes, it might be good to be a black-and-white whale with no enemies and only friends, but then, maybe it wouldn't be good," the spirit replied.

"Well, what about a lovely woman, with beautiful black hair and a musical laugh and a voluptuous form. What about a woman so lovely and kind that all who look at her are filled with joy and happiness, and whose cooking-pot is always filled with the finest of meats and whose lodge is always warm and cozy. Would you like that?" Raven asked.

"Why, yes. I would love to be loved and beautiful and have enough to eat and be an inspiration to others," the spirit said. "That would be good."

Raven smiled, and started to prepare a form for the lost one, happy that it had finally made a decision.

"But wait, Human Beings age, and that is not good. No, I don't want to get old and weak and wrinkled, and lose my fabulous beauty. That is not good. No, I do not want to be a Human Being," the spirit said.

"Yes-no-yes-no," the spirit chanted, and its head started turning round and round, like a child's spinning top; then its whole body began to twirl, and as it spun, the winds stirred, and Raven feared that another catastrophe would soon befall the village. The cooking pots, recently repaired and replaced on the cooking fires, started to rattle, and the flames of the cooking fires danced and swirled before the winds. Raven saw fear on the faces of the people who had come to him for help. He was also beginning to lose patience with the confused spirit.

"Stop it," Raven said. "You are scaring my creations, and making a mess."

"No-hope-no-hope. Yes-no-yes-no." The spirit twirled and whirled.

"I SAID STOP IT," Raven the Transformer, Raven the Shaman, Maker of Life and Keeper of Magic, yelled at the spirit. "Calm yourself. I have a solution to your problem, one that I know will make you and all of my creations happy. Trust in me, and hear my plan," Raven said, as he grabbed the frantic spirit and shook it.

"In a village not far from this one, there lives a dull-witted shaman. How he was able to become a shaman, an office that calls for great intelligence and care, is a mystery to me. A shaman must communicate and merge with the spirit-world. A shaman must have knowledge of healing plants and the herbs that I have placed upon the earth to help those in need. A shaman must be strong to overcome evil spirits and drive them out of a sick patient.

"This man does not know the ways of plants. Whenever he calls to the spirits, he forgets their names. He does not undertake curing of the sick for fear that he will kill the patient. He has little character and his soul is tiny as a nut-shell. You can take his body. Through you, predictions can be made; you will have healing powers and weather powers. You can transform into the body of this shaman, and his soul will merge with yours—it is so tiny and weak, you will hardly notice it. You will regain the esteem and love of the village people for their incompetent shaman."

The spirit stopped twirling, and the winds died down. "Oh, yes-yes-yes," the spirit said. "Happy-happy-happy. Love-love-love. Food-food-food. I will accept this gift from you, Raven."

Raven wrapped his wings around the spirit and the pair flew to the village of the incompetent shaman. Raven and the spirit waited in the trees outside the shaman's lodge until the dead of night, when the shaman would be asleep and his body most vulnerable to a takeover from the spirit world. After all, even through the shaman was an incompetent buffoon, he was still trained in spirit-ways and communication, and Raven did not want any resistance to his plan, however weak it might be.

In the dead of night, when the stars were shining bright-est and the hoot-hoot-hoot of the owl echoed through the darkness, Raven made his move. Raven and the spirit entered the sleeping shaman's lodge. Raven tipped the shaman's head back and opened his mouth.

"Hurry, get in, merge with his soul and assume his shape; you will be known as a great shaman and a friend to the people. Get in," Raven said.

"Oh, I don't know-know-know," whined the spirit. "He's

not as handsome as I want to be. I don't know-know-know."

"Get in there. If you don't like it, you can leave and we will find you another form," Raven hissed. "Just get in there."

The spirit entered the shaman's mouth and merged with his body and soul. When the spirit awoke the next morning, he whirled and twirled, ecstatic at having found and accepted a human form. Whirling and dancing, the shaman-spirit went from his lodge into his village. His people were overcome with amazement.

"Come and see our shaman," people called to each other. "Something wondrous has happened. Our shaman has been overtaken by a powerful spirit—a spirit that can give us answers to our questions and help us fulfill our lives."

Indeed, when a man prepared his kayak for fishing, he went to the shaman and asked if he would suc-ceed in his fishing. "Yes-yes-yes, there will be big schools of cod and halibut today; cast your net and you will bring home a feast of fish," the spirit-shaman said. "But on the other hand, there may not be many fish in the sea today, so don't be surprised if your catch is small or you find nothing."

Seal-hunters asked the spirit-shaman if

he would intercede with Sedna, a gigantic seal and Great Goddess, and ask her to help them with the hunt. The spirit-shaman spoke with Sedna and people asked, "Well, what did she say? Will we catch seals tomorrow?"

"Yes-yes-yes, you will catch many fine, fat seals," the spirit-shaman said. "But perhaps not, perhaps you may come home empty-handed. But try."

Thus, the transformed shaman never made a false prophecy. His people came to love him, and his fame and fortune grew far and wide. The spirit-shaman loved the people, and all of the spirits and the gods, and he never forgot Raven. He made prayers to Raven every day, thanking him for his kindness, compassion, and understanding.

The
Raven
Mocker*

Cherokee

A young man had been out on a hunting trip and was on his way home when night came on. He was still a long distance from the settlement but knew of a house not far off the trail where an old man and his wife lived. Turning in that direction to look for a place to sleep until morning, he found the house, but there was no one there.

Perhaps they have gone for water, he said to himself, and then stretched out in the farthest corner to sleep. Very soon he heard a raven cry outside, and a little while afterwards the old man came in and sat down by the fire without noticing the young man, who kept still in the dark corner. Soon there was another raven cry outside and the old man said, "Now my wife is coming."

Sure enough, the old woman came in and sat down by her husband. Then the young man knew they were Raven Mockers and he was frightened and kept very quiet. The old man asked his wife if she had been lucky with her night's hunting. The wife said, "No, there were too many doctors watching. What luck did you have?"

Her husband responded that he had gotten what he went for, and he reached into a pouch and brought out some meat and asked his wife to cook it so they could both eat. In a little while, the young man smelled something really delicious. He peeked and saw what looked like a human heart roasting on a spit over the fire.

"Who is over in the corner?" the old woman asked her husband. The old man said no one was there. But the woman insisted that they were not alone.

"I hear him snoring," the old witch said as she stirred the fire. The fire blazed and lit up the whole room, but the young hunter kept quiet and pretended to be asleep and oblivious to all that had happened. Finally, the old man shook him, and the hunter rubbed his eyes, as if waking from a deep sleep. By this time it was near daylight, and the old woman left the room to go and fix breakfast. The hunter heard the old woman cry as she prepared the meal. He asked the old man why his wife was sad.

The old man explained that his wife was sad because she

had lost some of her friends recently. But the hunter knew
she was crying because she feared she had been discovered for
what she really was—a witch.

When it was time to eat, the hunter was offered a bowl of
corn mush.

"This is all we have—we have had no meat for a long
time," the old man said.

The hunter ate the mush and started on his way home.
The old man came running behind him and offered him
some beautiful wampum beadwork, insisting that the youth
take it. The old man asked the hunter not to mention the
argument between him and his wife over whether or not there
was someone in their house.

"We are always quarreling that way," the old wizard said.

The hunter accepted the beads, but threw them into the
first creek he came across, and returned to his home village.
There he recited the whole adventure, and a war party went
with him to kill the Raven Mockers.

The warriors reached the house in the forest seven days
after the hunter first discovered the Raven Mockers. Finding
the old man and his wife lying dead in the house, the war
party set fire to the house and burned the witches together.

---

*From the beginning, there have been good and evil as well as power-
ful healers—medicine people and doctors. There have also been wizards
and witches, those who chose evil, those who caused pain and suffering
to enrich themselves. To the Cherokee, the most horrifying of these
evil-doers were known as *Kalanu Ahyeli ski,* "Raven Mockers." These

most powerful of sorcerers robbed the ill or dying of their lives, adding these years to their own. After killing their victim, Raven Mockers cut out the victim's heart and ate it; no one could see them and their knives left no scar. There was, however, medicine even against these most powerful agents of evil; strong doctors, good medicine people, were relied upon by the Cherokee when a loved one fell ill. If such a medicine person remained beside a sick person, Raven Mockers were afraid to enter the patient's house. If the patient died, the medicine man stayed with the body until it was buried, because Raven Mockers could not steal a heart after a proper burial.

TRANSITION AND TRANSFORMATION
Shaman's World

he indigenous peoples of North America integrated all aspects of nature into their daily lives. Hundreds of distinct cultures and languages developed among the tribes of North and South America, and despite many differences in cultural ethos, the ways that people viewed the world and their place in it, common themes—especially those having to do with religion and identity—were land-based. In North America, human beings considered themselves as part of the world; they considered themselves children of the Great Mother Earth, related to all denizens of the planet. Each animal, plant, and person had an important role to play in this cosmos. Among most tribes, the crow was an important messenger.

In 1492, the year when Europeans officially discovered America, the tribal world was on the brink of a transformation that would forever change the world of indigenous American and migrating European alike. European kings and queens expanded their empires and new nations—United States, Canada, and Mexico—were built upon the ruins of native cultures.

The stories of contact, transition, and transformation are as varied as the people who relate them. In some instances, contacts between Native American and European were welcomed and beneficial to both cultures; in others, contact resulted in the worst forms of aggression and brutality by both sides. The Columbia Plateau tribes and the Rocky Mountain tribes have always produced great prophets and mystic leaders, and among the Coeur d'Alene people of northern Idaho, it was said that crows and ravens told the people about the coming of the White Men. The prophecies of Circling Raven stood out among these visions, and opened the way for a peaceful contact between Red and White.

Other tribes did not fare as well. The mystic warriors of the plains—the Lakota, the Cheyenne, the Arapaho, and many others—found themselves facing overwhelming odds as their main food supply, the buffalo, was deliberately decimated by the Americans in an attempt to destroy the Indians whose lands they coveted. These closing chapters in the Indian wars are well-documented, both in formal Euro-American histories and in indigenous oral traditions.

During the 1880s and 1890s, many Indian people wondered if their children and grandchildren would survive the onslaught, while the United States government was certain that Native Americans stood on the brink of extinction. They asked soldiers, scholars, and others to document the death throes of what they assumed was a dying race.

In the fall of 1890, a young man of Celtic descent, James Mooney, was preparing to leave the Eastern seaboard for Indian

Territory. Mooney, a researcher with the United States Bureau
of Ethnology, had been instructed to go and live among the
Western tribes, to learn their languages and cultural ways.
Policy-makers in Washington, D.C., had heard rumors about
a militaristic revitalization movement sweeping through the
Great Basin and across the plains, one that incited Indian people to pray for the destruction of the Whites and the forma-
tion of a new world order. Mooney was asked to investigate
this, and the result was one of the most remarkable explana-
tions of an important religion ever written.

Mooney was the son of parents who had fled their Irish
homeland due to British oppression. His Celtic heart must
have responded when he learned the message of the new religion, which was to pray and dance for a better world, a world
of beauty and justice, a world free from oppression. The
religion originated in Nevada with a Paiute prophet named
Wovoka, who was called "the Father" by his disciples. Mooney
learned about it from Arapaho and Cheyenne friends and was
inspired by the message; he himself danced the Father's dance.
He travelled to Nevada to meet the prophet himself, and
spent more than three years living among the Western tribes,
learning various interpretations of the prophet's words.
Through Mooney's eyes, and the words of the prophet and
his followers, the most detailed information about the religion has been preserved. (Despite Mooney's attempts to explain
the faith, the federal governments of the United States and
Canada outlawed the Father's Dance and many other aspects
of indigenous religions until well into the twentieth century.)

Mooney met Wovoka at the prophet's home on New Year's Day 1892. Wovoka's camp was covered in deep snow. Guided by Wovoka's uncle, Mooney entered Wovoka's house, an open-centered hut made of tule rushes. A fire blazed in the middle of the hut, and Wovoka was surrounded by members of his family, "consisting of his young wife, a boy about four years of age, of whom he [Wovoka] seemed very fond, and an infant. It was plain that he was a kind husband and father, which was in keeping with his reputation among the whites for industry and reliability. . . ." (MOONEY, 1893)

Wovoka asked Mooney why he wanted an interview. He told Mooney that many people had lied about his visions and his message, that much trouble had resulted, and since the white people seemed determined to misunderstand his words, perhaps it would be better if he said nothing. Wovoka's uncle interceded on Mooney's behalf, explaining that Mooney had learned about the dance from Cheyennes and Arapahoes who had come to Wovoka to learn the doctrine, and that Mooney himself had danced the dance.

Wovoka proceeded to ask Mooney many questions about his Arapaho and Cheyenne friends, and said he was happy to learn that Mooney was close to these people. Mooney showed Wovoka pictures of his Arapaho friend, Black Coyote, who had taught Mooney the dance, and had visited with Wovoka and learned it directly from the prophet. Assured of Mooney's sincerity, Wovoka then spoke freely. He explained the doctrine to Mooney, and told him his message of peace, brotherhood, and world renewal.

"He makes no claim to be Christ, the Son of God, as has so often been asserted in print," Mooney wrote. "He does claim to be a prophet who has received a divine revelation.... He made no arguments and advanced no proofs, but said simply that he had been with God, as though the statement no more admitted of controversy than the proposition that two and two are four." (MOONEY, 1893)

Mooney asked Wovoka if he could photograph him. Wovoka said that his photograph had never been made and he was reluctant to pose, but he told Mooney that since he had travelled all the way from Washington, D.C., especially to learn about him and his doctrine, and since Mooney had friends among the tribes, he must be a good man, and agreed to the photo session.

Mooney told Wovoka he would show his picture to his Indian friends, and he bought some things from Wovoka's family to give to these friends. Mooney obtained "a blanket of rabbit skins, some piñon nuts, some tail feathers of the magpie, highly prized by the Paiutes for ornamentation, and some of the sacred red paint, endowed with miraculous powers, which plays so important a part in the ritual of the Ghost Dance religion. Then, with mutual expressions of good will, we parted, his uncle going back to the reservation, while I took the train for Indian territory. . . ." (MOONEY, 1893)

Clearly impressed by Wovoka and his religion, Mooney urged Washington bureaucrats, politicians, and soldiers to leave the religion and its devotees alone. In writing about it he said:

"The moral code inculcated is as pure and comprehensive in its simplicity as anything found in religious
systems from the days of Gautaama Buddha to the
time of Jesus Christ. Do no harm to any one. Do
right always. Could anything be more simple, and yet
more exact and exacting? It inculcates honesty: Do
not tell lies. It preaches good will: Do no harm to
anyone. It forbids the extravagant mourning customs
formerly common among the tribes: When your
friends die, you must not cry, which is interpreted by
the prairie tribes as forbidding the killing of horses,
the burning of tipis, and destruction of property, the
cutting off of the hair, and the gashing to the body
with knives, all of which were formerly the sickening
rule at every death until forbidden by the new doctrine. As an Arapaho said to me when his little boy
died, 'I shall not shoot any ponies, and my wife will
not gash her arms. We used to do this when our
friends died, because we thought we would never see
them again, and it made us feel bad. But now we
know that we shall all be united again. . . .' "
(MOONEY, 1893)

Above all, Wovoka's doctrine prohibited war. Mooney
explained that it was difficult for Euro-Americans to fully
comprehend what "tremendous and radical change. . .this
doctrine works in the whole spirit of savage life." Mooney
pointed out that war is the career of every prairie Indian.

"His proudest title has been that of warrior. His conversation by day and his dreams by night have been of bloody deeds upon the enemies of his tribe. His highest boast was in the number of his scalp trophies, and his chief delight at home was in the war dance and the scalp dance. . . .Now comes a prophet as a messenger from God to forbid not only war, but all that savors of war—the war dance, the scalp dance, and even the bloody torture of the sun dance—and his teaching is accepted and his words obeyed by four-fifths of all the warlike, predatory tribes of the mountains and in the great plains. Only those who have known the deadly hatred that once animated Ute, Cheyenne, and Pawnee, one toward another, and are able to contrast it with their present spirit of brotherly love, can know what the Ghost Dance religion has accomplished. . . .It is such a revolution as comes but once in the life of a race."
(MOONEY, 1893)

Despite Mooney's accurate portrayal of the religion, spirit dancers were persecuted, even killed, by white soldiers. In 1890, the United States military massacred Lakota ghost dancers at Wounded Knee, and more were buried in the graves of Chief Big Foot and his murdered children than was first realized. Soldiers who killed the innocent were awarded Congressional Medals of Honor and the conscience of a nation was buried in the frozen, bloody ground of Wounded Knee. For Native Americans, the closing decade of the nineteenth century was an era of bereavement and grief. Wovoka's dance offered balm for physical, psychic, and spiritual wounds—a mechanism for coping and a prescription for survival.

Ghost dancers believed that Crow carried their prayers and supplications. They danced so that their people would survive, so that their children would have a future. The omniscient Crow listened to the prayers, and fulfilling the duties of a messenger, conveyed them to Heaven.

A new synthesis arose from the clashes and confrontations. Increasingly, Americans realized that the land and the people were one. Native beliefs, ancient European tribal totems, the rise of American Romanticism, the turning of mainstream Americans to nature religions and the environmental movements: the shaman's world flowed into the modern world.

The Prophecies
of Circling Raven

*I*n the lake country of northern Idaho, nestled among
the foothills of the Rockies, lies the land of a Salishan
people known today as the Coeur d'Alene. Before the coming
of the White Man, they called themselves the Skitswish. One
of their greatest leaders was a chief who acquired the name
of Circling Raven, and whose memory has been cherished by
his people through the generations. Circling Raven was beloved
by the Bird People, especially Raven and Crow, because he
understood corvid languages and utilized the birds as advisors
and strategists. Through their gifts of prophecy, the birds
taught the chief many things, and acted as allies and guides to
the Coeur d'Alene. Chief Circling Raven's exploits and prophecy songs have been recited by his descendants for over two
hundred years and his story and the history of the Coeur
d'Alene people were written down in English by tribal historian
Chief Joseph Seltice in the 1940s; Seltice was schooled in the
oral history and cultural traditions of his people, and compiled
the first comprehensive history of the Skitswish.

According to Seltice, the Skitswish nation consisted of five
hundred people in the year 1740, and their headman was the

prophet Circling Raven, who acquired his adult name after
leading a hunting party over the Rocky Mountains and into
buffalo country. Their hunger for buffalo meat led the Skitswish
into enemy Blackfeet territory, but through the wise counsel
of Raven, they prevailed over their enemies and returned to
their lodges with delectable fresh buffalo for the winter.

"There had been trouble between the Coeur d'Alene,
Sioux [Crows/Absorka], and Blackfeet Indians of Montana
over the millions of buffalo roaming the plains of Montana,"
Seltice wrote. "By territorial rights, the buffalo did belong to
the Montana tribes of Indians; the Coeur d'Alenes were trespassers." According to Seltice, in 1760, one hundred Coeur
d'Alene braves and their families followed their chief into the
buffalo country.

"After crossing the divide into the plains of Montana,
[they] encamped. . .for some days, as [the chief] had scouts
out to locate the whereabouts of the buffalo. . . .In the
prophecy of songs, he told his people to listen. 'There are three
ravens coming over to give us news.' In just a few minutes,
three ravens circled the encampment and gave out three caws.
He asked his people if they understood. His people told him,
'No, we do not understand birds.' [The chief] told his people,
'The Raven said, "you have an enemy who already spied you
and [is] preparing for an attack, therefore, prepare yourselves.
As far as I can see, there is already bloodshed on the enemy
side of seven. When you count seven wounded or dead, with-
draw, because then there will be bloodshed on our side [if you
press your advantage]. Beware and follow this." ' "

Shortly after the message of the Raven was translated, a

battle ensued between the buffalo-hungry Skitswish and the
Absorka and their allies. The Skitswish obeyed the instructions
of Raven, and withdrew after wounding seven Absorka warriors. Not one of their own people was wounded.

"Thus the name of Circling Raven was inherited by a
Coeur d'Alene chief living in the year 1740," Seltice wrote.
"At this time, he was right in the prime of his life, at the age
of one hundred and fifty years, in perfect health, with upright
command of his people. The prophecy of this battle [made
him] the man of the hour."

After the battle, the Skitswish located a huge buffalo herd
and the hunters killed many, packed some fresh meat, dried
and smoked the rest, and started their journey back to their
homeland with a train of two hundred pack animals. The
successful hunting party ran into difficulties on their return
trip, however, when an early blizzard trapped them in the
Bitterroot Mountains.

"The snow was between fifteen and twenty feet in depth
for several miles; this being impassable, there was no one to
turn to but Circling Raven," Seltice wrote. Circling Raven
prayed his prayers and sang his prophecy songs, and despite
the inclement weather, the people were happy, because there
was so much buffalo meat to eat. Their main concern was
finding fodder for their ponies, as the depth of the snow prevented the ponies from pawing through to the grass.

After one night of praying and singing, Circling Raven's
medicine prevailed. A warm wind began to blow; it blew for
two full days and nights, melting the snow and opening the
mountain passes into the Skitswish homeland.

It was typical for the Coeur d'Alenes, like other Columbia Plateau and western Rocky Mountain groups, to spend spring and summer in the cool highlands and winter in the comparative warmth of the river valleys whose waters fed into the Clearwater, Snake, and mighty Columbia rivers. The tribe spent the winter of 1740 at the confluence of two such rivers, a place Seltice calls Kingston. It was here at Kingston, during the traditional observance of the winter solstice, that Raven and Crow revealed something wonderful to Circling Raven.

Raven and Crow told the prophet-chief that long, long ago, in a land far away, a savior of the world was born on Solstice Night. Circling Raven listened to the revelations of the Bird People, and told his people that on the night of winter solstice, they should include the remembrance of this savior's birth in their prayers. He further said that at this time all young children and babies should be fed extra delicacies, and that, in honor of this savior, his people and even the enemies of the Skitswish should not fight with each other during the period immediately before and after the solstice.

On Solstice Day 1740, Circling Raven told his people that Raven had revealed something even more amazing. He said that Raven told him that within a hundred years, men would come to his homeland with news of this savior. These men would be clothed in long black robes, fulfilling "the prophecy of one hundred years, coming of the Black Robes, to teach us only the truth and the real occurrence of the birth of the savior into this world." (SELTICE)

From solstice 1740 until the end of his days, Circling Raven waited and searched for the Black Robes, sending runners and scouts to look for them. He waited twenty years, truly expecting the arrival of the people who would give him all the details about this savior born long ago. In the end, Circling Raven never saw the Black Robes, or heard the stories about the savior from their lips. Raven and Crow taught him all he knew about the savior, and Circling Raven in turn taught his son Twisted Earth about the savior and how to talk with the Bird People.

When Twisted Earth was twelve years old, his father told him that he feared that he himself would not live long enough to see the Black Robes, but that surely the boy would. He said that after his death, his son should await the coming of these Black Robes and lead his people to them. Circling Raven died in the winter of 1760, and his people ". . .mournfully buried him at Kingston, the country he loved so much. His favorite mountain of all was the Old Grizzly west of Kingston, where the meat, fish, and fruit were plentiful. . . ." (SELTICE)

Following his father's instructions, Twisted Earth led the tribe and continued the search for the mysterious Black Robes.

"This boy Twisted Earth roamed the mountains east of Kingston, opposite his father's stomping grounds. . .in the vicinity of the Little North Fork of the Clearwater. . . .He would approach the Bitterroot Valley in Montana in search of the Black Robes year after year. . .never losing patience, but in confidence of his father's prophecy of the coming of the Black Robes. . . .He sang the joyous songs of prophecy and continued the solstice celebrations as his father had instructed." (SELTICE)

In about the year 1780, after a buffalo hunt on friendly terms with the Montana tribes, Twisted Earth, by then forty-two, celebrated solstice with his people at Kingston. During the evening's festivities, Twisted Earth told his people, "Listen, a raven and a crow are coming to give us news." His tribesmen said they were surprised that birds would come during mid-winter, and in the night. They asked Twisted Earth from where the birds were coming. Twisted Earth said, "They are sent to give us news, whether it is winter, summer, spring or fall." (SELTICE)

The winter songs of prophecy were sung in a large, rectangular, bark lodge. On solstice night the lodge was crowded with people, and Twisted Earth told his tribesmen to prepare a perch for Crow and Raven. Three fires burned in the long house, one at each end and one in the middle. After a small pole with a strong rope perch was prepared for the birds, Twisted Earth told the people, "Listen, they are coming; see that the pole is fastened up there tight for them to sit on." After everyone had checked the perch, two birds flew in, a raven and a crow.

The prophecy song was sung,

"the mournful lyrics taken in by the birds, grave in manner, both sitting on a pole close to the top of the lodge. In some two hours, much smoke circled to the top of the large lodge; the two birds blinked their eyes. . . . Twisted Earth, seeing this, said, 'It's time for the birds to go.' The birds flapped their wings and

[said], 'Caw, caw, caw,' then flew out from on top of
the lodge, the way they flew in." (SELTICE)

Twisted Earth asked his people, "Did you understand the birds?"
As they had long ago, his people said, "No, we do not understand birds." Twisted Earth conveyed the message of Raven.

"Raven said that we won't see the Black Robes for sixty
years, but [do not] lose patience, your. . .celebration is accurate, a pleasing assemblage to the Creator who was born a
baby into this world long, long ago."

Twisted Earth and his people continued their search and
their wait for the Black Robes. They searched in the land of
the Flathead Indians. They searched the Bitterroot Valley,
near what is now Missoula, Montana. Every summer, Twisted
Earth scoured the Bitterroots, a determined man who never
lost faith in his father's prophecies. Each July, Twisted Earth
returned "to his father's favorite stomping grounds, the Old
Grizzly Mountain, for huckleberries and a meat supply of
brown bear. After the hunt on Old Grizzly, he would tramp
the mountains of the little north fork of the Clearwater River
for a salmon supply, then into the neighborhood of the White
Mountains. . .for elk and deer. . . ."

One year, elk were so abundant in the White Mountains
that the Skitswish did not need to go over the mountains into
buffalo country on the annual hunt. There were so many elk
and so many salmon that the winter food supply was assured.
"Salmon was hooked out of the headwaters of the north fork
as fast as a man could throw; all game and fish were dried and

smoked by the women before starting home." (SELTICE)

After realizing how great Earth's bounty was in this season, the Coeur d'Alenes elected to stay in their own country and not take the buffalo trail. They discussed the coming of the Black Robes at great length with their friends the Flatheads— in the tradition of the inland-mountain tribes, other prophets had shared the vision of Black Robes coming to the homelands of the Flathead, the Pend d'Oreille, the Kalispel, and the Kootenai. A famous Kootenai shaman named Shining Shirt prophesied Black Robes and the teachings of a God-man these Black Robes represented.

By the 1830s, all the tribes were aware of Protestant missionary activities in the Oregon country, but the Flatheads and the Coeur d'Alenes were unimpressed with these missionaries and wanted Black Robes. In addition to the prophecies from the Bird People, Mohawk refugees had come among the mountain tribes with information about their own experiences with the Black Robes. As a result of the prophecies and the information from the Mohawks, the tribes sent three delegations to the far-away city of St. Louis. Details of the delegations are described in letters between Father Joseph Rosati of St. Louis and the Father General of the Society of Jesus in Rome.

> "Eight or nine years ago [about 1830], some of the Flathead nation came to St. Louis. The object of their journey was to ascertain if the religion spoken of with so much praise by the Iroquois warriors was in reality such as represented, and above all, if the nations that

have white skin [name they give to Europeans] had adopted and practiced it. Soon after their arrival in St. Louis, they fell sick, called for the priest, and earnestly asked by signs to be baptized. Their request was eagerly granted and they received the holy baptism with great devotion; then holding the crucifix, they covered it with affectionate kisses and expired. Later [about 1832], the Flathead nation. . .sent one of the Iroquois to St. Louis. . . .He asked missionaries for his countrymen, and started with the hope that one day, the desire of the nation would be at last accomplished. But on his journey he was killed by the infidel Indians of the Sioux nation.

"At last, a third deputation of Indians arrived at St. Louis in 1839 after a long voyage of three months. It was composed of two Christian Iroquois. . . .I rejoiced with them at their happiness and gave them the hope to have soon a priest.

"They will leave tomorrow for their home; a priest will follow them next Spring. Out of the twenty-four Iroquois who formerly emigrated from Canada, four only are still living. Not content with planting the Faith in these savage countries, they have also defended it against the prejudices of the Protestant ministers. When these pretended missionaries presented themselves, our good Catholics refused to receive them. 'These are not the priests we have spoken of to you,' they said to the Flatheads, 'they are not the priests with

> long black gowns, who have no wives, who say Mass,
> and carry a crucifix with them,' etc. For God's sake,
> my Right Rev. Father, forsake not their souls. . . ."

The letter evoked a quick response from the Jesuits, the Counter-Reformation's Catholic Soldiers for Christ. Father John De Smet was chosen to go to the Flathead and their Salishan brothers, the Coeur d'Alene. He left St. Louis in 1840 and had such an enthusiastic reception among the Flatheads that he returned to St. Louis and asked for more priests in 1841. In two months among the Flatheads, he converted over six hundred people. The Jesuits assigned two other priests to De Smet's mission, and they all returned to the lake country.

The prophecy of Circling Raven was fulfilled on June 2, 1842, when De Smet entered the homeland of the Skitswish. He was spotted at what is now called Post Falls, Idaho, by three of Twisted Earth's scouts. He and his group were taken to Twisted Earth's lodge at the headwaters of the Spokane River, where the modern city of Coeur d'Alene lies today, on Skitswish land.

Twisted Earth was overwhelmed by the prophecy's fulfillment. When De Smet and his associate Father Mengarini were led into the chief's lodge, there was a long silence. Twisted Earth said he was filled with a mixture of joy and sorrow, and tears streamed down his face. He was happy that the priests had finally arrived, but saddened because his father was not alive to see them.

"My father looked for you for a long time," Twisted
Earth told the Jesuits. "Many years he searched the
entire Bitterroot Valley. Many times beyond the divide
he travelled, until in old age, he asked me to extend
the lookout for the Black Robes. It has been fully a
hundred years since my father started singing the
prophecy song, 'Coming of the Black Robes.' When
he died, I continued the watch for the Black Robes.
Now, after eighty years of crossing the mountains,
looking throughout the Bitterroot Valley, and following my father's footsteps many times beyond the
divide, today the goal was reached." (SELTICE)

The Skitswish welcomed the Jesuits, and De Smet fulfilled a
long-awaited prophecy. Largely through their relationship
with the Jesuits and the Skitswish, Circling Raven's people
were spared many of the horrors that other tribes experienced
at the hands of the Americans.

Crow and
the Ghost Dance

Because I am poor,
Because I am poor,
I pray for every living creature,
I pray for every living creature.

KIOWA GHOST DANCE SONG

By 1890, the land of North America had been claimed by alien invaders. Cycles of European conquest initiated in 1492 were completed, and as the land suffered, her children cried out to heaven. From the arid wastelands of Nevada arose a prophet; Heaven gave him visions and instructed him in ways to release Mother Earth and free her children from the yoke of oppression, exploitation, and destruction.

The prophet was a Paiute named Wovoka, "The Cutter." God taught him a prayer-dance to rejuvenate the Earth and revitalize her people. Euro-Americans called this prayer for restoration "The Ghost Dance." The bureaucrats in Washington, D.C., feared it, as did their Canadian counterparts, because they did not understand Wovoka's doctrine.

The prophet's prayer-dance swept out of Nevada across the

Rocky Mountains and into the Great Plains, stirring the souls of people from the Pacific Coast to the Mississippi River. From California to Missouri, devotees danced; in some instances, white and red people danced together in prayer for the return of the buffalo and a restoration of Nature, the ancient Mother. Wovoka continued the prophetic traditions of his father, Tavibo, whose name in Paiute means "White Man."* Tavibo was a tribal chief and a prophetic dreamer who instructed his son in shamanic ways; his visions never evoked the pan-Indian response that his son's did, however.

Wovoka was reported to have begun receiving visions during his adolescence in the 1860s, but his greatest revelation occurred toward the end of the 1880s, and it was this that gave rise to his messianic mission.

On this occasion "the sun died" (was eclipsed) and Wovoka fell asleep and "was taken up to the other world."

> "Here he saw God, with all of the people who had
> died long ago engaged in their oldtime sports and
> occupations, all happy and forever young. It was a
> pleasant land and full of game. After showing him all,

*The exact genetic relationship between Wovoka and Tavibo evoked much speculation by non-Indians. Some wondered whether Tavibo was the genetic father, an uncle, or a spiritual father. Wovoka said Tavibo was his father, and after his father's death he was taken into the family of the Anglo farmer Jack Wilson. After the death of his paternal grandfather, Wovoka assumed his grandfather's name, *Kwohitsauq*, "Big Rumbling Belly." Thus, Wovoka is remembered by three names: Wovoka, Kwohitsauq, and Jack Wilson. After his ascent to religious dominance, Paiute and other devotees called him "our father."

God told him he must go back and tell his people they must be good and love one another, have no quarreling and live in peace with the whites; that they must work and not lie or steal; that they must put away all of the old practices that savored of war; that if they faithfully obeyed his instructions they would at last be reunited with their friends in this other world, where there would be no more death or sickness or old age.

"He was then given the dance which he was commanded to bring back to his people. By performing this dance at intervals, for five consecutive days each time, they would secure this happiness for themselves and hasten the event.

"Finally God gave him control over the elements so that he could make it rain or snow or be dry at will, and appointed him his deputy to take charge of affairs in the west, while Governor Harrison [referring to the United States President Harrison] would attend to matters in the east, and he, God, would look after the world above. He then returned to the earth and began to preach as he was directed, convincing the people

by exercising the wonderful powers that had been
given him."   (MOONEY, 1892-1893)

The Father's Dance was a supplication for survival and renewal. Prior to dancing, participants had to cleanse themselves; the Lakota conducted a sweat-lodge ceremony before
their dances, as did other Prairie groups. They would then
dress in garments made of simple white cloth. Forming a
dance circle, men and woman alternated, holding hands with
the person on either side. In some observations, a pole, a fire,
or a cedar tree would be in the middle of the circle. Dances
lasted a total of five days—four successive nights and all night
until the morning of the fifth day, when all devotees would
then bathe and go home. Feasting also was a large part of the
observance, and many tribes developed special gambling
games to entertain themselves when taking breaks from the
dance. At the conclusion of a dance, medicine people and
dancers would shake blankets and banners to dispel bad influences and drive away sickness and disease.

As a messenger between this world and the Spirit World,
Crow was the sacred bird of the Ghost Dance, the essential
contact between the two worlds. The color black represented
the mysterious, and it was well-known that Crow and Raven
were medicine birds who could cross over to the Land of the
Dead to bring back messages from departed loved ones. On
occasion, they interceded to bring a soul back from the dark
land before the body had completely died.

Dancers wore crow feathers in their hair, painted crows on
their dancing clothes, and carried crows in dance circles; if a

devotee found the body of a crow, he or she would accept its remains as an honorable gift, preserve it, and bring it to the dance circle as well. Crow was called upon to hasten the revitalization of the world and the melding of the living world with the Spirit World.

Other birds were also honored in the dance: the eagle (important in all tribal ceremonies as carrier of prayers), the magpie (as relative to Crow and Raven, also because the black-and-white feather colors represented the world of the living and the dead together in one entity), and the sage-hen (in deference to the Paiute and the homeland of Wovoka). Crow, however, was the pivotal figure.

Sometimes, dancers referred to the crow as "Father," or "Mother," meaning that the divine Crow would be the one to gather up the hosts from the Spirit World and bring them into the new world after purification and renewal. In some societies, it was believed that Wovoka himself would metamorphose into a crow and lead the transformation. Medicine men and individual dancers composed songs about the coming renewal, and many of these songs were recorded by Mooney during his sojourn in the West. In one of these songs, Wovoka transformed into a crow and flew around the entire world to deliver his messianic message:

> My children, my children,
> I am flying about the earth,
> I am flying about the earth.
> I am a crow, my children,
> I am a crow, my children,

Says the father,
Says the father.

One of the Arapaho, a man named Little Raven who
travelled to see Wovoka in August of 1891, composed a song
urging devotees to prepare for the coming of the new world:

Stand ready, stand ready,
So that when the crow calls you,
So that when the crow calls you,
You will see him,
You will see him.

Another Arapaho song, discussing the preparations of the
crow for the coming world, goes like this:

The crow is making a road,
He is making a road,
He has finished it,
He has finished it.
His children,
His children,
He has brought them together,
He has brought them together.

This song celebrates the spirit-path that Crow has made,
calling all of the dead together, getting ready to bring them
out from the shadow-land into the new, beautiful world of
happiness and warm sunlight. The Arapaho believed that the

spirit world was in the West, on the same level as their world, but on mountains surrounded by water. Crow, a leader of the Spirit World and a messenger, collected the departed and brought them to the hills overlooking this sea. To the east of the sea of the dead was the boundary of the living world, where all of their relatives and descendants were dancing and waiting for them.

In an Arapaho story, Crow took a pebble in his beak, dropped it into the water, and it became a giant mountain, assisting the passage of the dead to the sea. Crow led the legions of the dead down to the seashore, and taking some dirt in his beak, flew out and dropped the dirt in the water, magically transforming the dirt into a causeway connecting the Spirit World to the Living World. Crow then flew away from the spirit-people, toward the East, to the Living Land. When he returned to the shadow-legions, he held blades of grass in his bill; he dropped these blades on the dirt causeway, and it was instantly covered with beautiful green sod. He flew to the East, and returned again, carrying twigs and leaves in his bill. He dropped these, and from the causeway sprang a beautiful forest of living trees. Crow flew to the base of the mountain he had made and supervised the passage of those in the Spirit World across his causeway and into the Living World, the world he was revitalizing.

The Arapaho song continues:

The earth—the crow,
The earth—the crow.

The crow brought it with him,
The crow brought it with him.

In one Arapaho song, the devotee saw a crow in a vision, and the crow told him to get ready to meet his lost loved ones, because he was bringing them back to earth. It was one of the most popular of the Arapaho ghost songs.

The crow is circling above me,
The crow is circling above me,
The crow has come for me,
The crow has come for me.

In another song, describing the meeting of the two worlds with Crow as transformer, Crow hands the new world to human beings:

My children!
My children!
Here it is, I hand it to you.
The earth!
The earth!

Like many tribes, the Arapaho believed that Crow saw all, and knew all that was, all that is, and all that will be. In the 1890s, an Arapaho band was reported to have cared for a hand-raised crow who was said to speak in the Arapaho language and to convey prophecies from the Spirit World to the Living World. This crow frequently appeared at Arapaho dance circles.

In Cheyenne songs, Crow brought the whirlwind that heralded the arrival of the spirits and the restoration of the world. Mo'ki, "Little Woman," a Cheyenne Ghost Dance leader, composed a number of songs about Crow, lord of both the spirit and the newly restored world. Mo'ki and her Arapaho husband Grant Left Hand* had lost their children, the first child soon after the little girl's birth, and the second, a little boy, at age four after a sudden illness. Through the Ghost Dance trance, Mo'ki visited her lost children, parents, and friends.

She converted Grant to the religion and he founded an auxiliary dance, the Arapaho "Crow Dance." During Grant's trance-visions, he reported seeing his children and riding with his little boy on a beautiful pony across the green prairies of the Spirit World.

By becoming Crow Woman, Mo'ki assumed the responsibilities of a female messenger from the Spirit World, belonging more to the Spirit World than to the world into which she was born. An important organizer of the Cheyenne and Arapaho ghost dances, she wrote many songs about the dance:

> The crow woman,
> The crow woman.
> To her home,
> To her home.
> She is going,
> She is going.
> She will see it,

---

*Grant Left Hand was a graduate of Carlisle Indian School and a son of *Nawat* (Left-Hand), a principal Arapaho chief.

She will see it.
Her children,
Her children.
She will see them,
She will see them.

Wovoka's doctrine was straightforward: the time would
come when all Indian peoples, living and dead, would be
reunited on a regenerated earth, to live a life of peace and
happiness, without oppression, forever free from death, hunger,
disease, and misery.

Through the medium of ritual dance, prayers for revitalization were delivered. To this basic foundation, each tribe added its own mythology and interpretation, and each devotee
added a part of himself or herself, with specific additions as
learned in the visionary trance. Wovoka sent out missionaries
to teach all people his dance, and both men and women had
equal participation in the rituals.

Wovoka taught that the revitalization would be a divine
occurrence, not man-made; by adhering to his doctrine, and
dancing the dance, however, Heaven would assist the devotees. He also stressed that the spiritual power which would
bring the rebirth needed no assistance from human beings—
it was inevitable.

"Though certain medicine-men were disposed to
anticipate the Indian millennium by preaching resistance to the further encroachments of the whites, such
teachings form no part of the true doctrine, and it was
only where chronic dissatisfaction was aggravated by

recent grievances, as among the Sioux, that the movement assumed a hostile expression. On the contrary,
all believers were exhorted to make themselves worthy
of the predicted happiness by discarding all things war-
like and practicing honesty, peace, and good will, not
only among themselves, but also towards the whites, so
long as they were together. Some apostles have even
thought that all race distinctions are to be obliterated,
and that the whites are to participate with the Indians
in the coming felicity." (MOONEY, 1892-93)

Word of Wovoka's visions spread quickly among the tribes.
Delegations came to his home in the Mason Valley, Nevada,
and representatives of the Arapaho, Cheyenne, and Lakota
came to see the gentle prophet and learn his doctrine and
dance. Some Paiutes went out to the tribes, carrying the message. A Paiute apostle brought the dance to the Hualapai of
northeastern Arizona in the spring of 1889; the Hopi and the
Navajo learned about it from the Pais, but did not embrace the
new religion, nor did the Absorka (Crow) of Montana, nor the
Skitswish of the Coeur d'Alene region or the Nez Perce of the
Columbia Plateau, although they were fully aware of the
messianic faith. However, the majority of tribes west of the
Mississippi did dance for the reawakening of the world.

One of the first apostles of Wovoka to bring the dance to
the prairie was the Cheyenne mystic Porcupine. Porcupine
and several companions crossed the Rockies in the fall of 1889
to discuss the religion with the prophet and to dance near

Walker Lake, Nevada. Porcupine explained his pilgrimage
months later to an American military officer. According to
him, Wovoka told Porcupine that in his great vision, he
ascended to heaven and talked to God, Father of All:

> "My father told me the earth was getting old and
> worn out and the people getting bad, and that I was
> to renew everything as it used to be and make it better,"
> Wovoka explained to Porcupine. "He also told us that
> all our dead were to be resurrected; that they were all
> to come back to earth, and that, as the earth was too
> small for them and us, he would do away with heaven
> and make the earth itself large enough to contain us
> all; that we must tell the people that we meet about
> these things. He spoke to us about fighting, and said
> that was bad and we must keep from it; that the earth
> was to be all good hereafter, and we must all be
> friends with one another.
>
> "He said that. . .the youth of all good people would
> be renewed, so that nobody would be more than forty
> years old. . . .He said that if we were all good he would
> send people among us who could heal all our wounds
> and sickness by mere touch and that we would live for-
> ever. He told us not to quarrel or fight or strike each
> other, or shoot one another; that the whites and Indians
> were to be all one people. He said that if any man dis-
> obeyed what he ordered, his tribe would be wiped from
> the face of the earth. . . . " (MOONEY, 1892-93)

Porcupine's description of his travels explained how he and his friends travelled by horse, rail, and wagon to the Mason Valley, and how he made friends with tribal representatives of Snakes, Bannocks, Shoshone, and Paiutes, whom he called "Fish-Eaters." He said he experienced great kindness from both Indian and white people, and described Anglos dancing and praying along with Indians.

> "I will tell you about it," Porcupine explained to Major Carroll at the Tongue River Agency, Montana, on June 15, 1890. "I want you all to listen to this so that there will be no mistake. There is no harm in what I am to say to anyone. I heard this where I met my friends in Nevada. It is a wonder you [white] people never heard this before. In the dance we had there [Nevada] the whites and Indians danced together. I met there a great many kinds of people, but they all seemed to know all about this religion. The people there seemed all to be good. I never saw any drinking or fighting or bad conduct among them. They treated me well, [let me travel] on the [railroad] cars without pay. They gave me food without charge, and I found that this was a habit among them toward their neighbors. I thought it strange that the people there should have been so good, so different from those here.... I and my people have been living in ignorance until I went and found out the truth. All the whites and Indians are brothers, I was told there. I never knew this before. . ." (MOONEY, 1892-93)

Wovoka's doctrine had many names, depending upon the
tribal groups that adopted it. Among the Paiutes, it was called
Nanigukwa, "dance in a circle," because men and women
stood together in a circle, holding hands and dancing. The
Shoshone called it *Tamana rayara*, "everybody dragging," because people stood and danced in a circle, and sometimes
shuffled their feet like children do in their ring games. The
Comanche called it *Apanekara*, "the Father's Dance," or
sometimes, "the dance with joined hands." The Kiowa called
it *Manposoti guan*, "dance with clasped hands." The Caddo
called it *Aakakimbawiut*, "the prayer of all to the Father." But
the Lakota, Arapaho, and most of the other prairie tribes called
it the "spirit" or "ghost" dance, because everything connected
to it related to rebirth and the return of the lost, and it is by
this name it is remembered.

Each tribe also had slightly different interpretations
about how and when the great transformation would occur.
East of the Rockies, it was believed that the faithful would fall
into a deep sleep, the earth would shake, and they would
awaken to immortality in a new world. Most tribes, including
the Shoshone of Wyoming, believed that this sleep would last
four days and four nights, and that on the morning of the
fifth day, when the dreamers awoke, they would behold a
new world where all creatures would dwell in happiness and
peace forever.

"The Cheyenne, Arapaho, Kiowa, and others of
Oklahoma say that the new earth, with all the resur-
rected dead from the beginning, and with the buffalo,

the elk, and other game upon it, will come from the
west and slide over the present earth, as the right hand
might slide over the left. As it approaches, the Indians
will be carried upward and alight on it by the aid of
the sacred dance feathers [feathers of the crow, the
spiritual messenger] which they wear in their hair and
which will act as wings to bear them up. They will then
become unconscious for four days, and on waking out
of their trance will find themselves with their former
friends in the midst of all the old-time surroundings."
(MOONEY, 1882)

The Arapaho apostle Sitting Bull (not to be confused with
the Lakota shaman) said that the new world would be pre-
ceded by a wall of fire, which would drive the Europeans
back to their native lands across the ocean, "to their original
and proper country." While this fire drove away the invaders,
the Indians, through the sacred dance-feathers of the crow,
would rise above the flames and cross them into the new world.

The Lakota added a particularly militaristic slant to Wovoka's
doctrine, which is understandable given the prestigious role
of war and coup-counting in Lakota society. This pride in
honorable warfare, coupled with the extreme abuses the Lakota
suffered at the hands of the United States government and
many of the whites who moved into the Black Hills at the
mere hint of a gold discovery, added new dimensions to the
Ghost Dance religion. Much of the United States government's fear about the religion was a result of federal misinter-

pretation of Lakota misinterpretations of the Father's Dance.

The Lakota were dissatisfied about the continued erosion of their land base by the United States government, the loss of their buffalo, and the refusal of the United States Congress to deliver food and cattle guaranteed them by treaty terms. As a result, their interpretation of the Ghost Dance was far more aggressive and war-like than Wovoka's visions dictated.

A report dated October 17, 1890, by Standing Rock Sioux Agent James McLaughlin, detailed the coming millennium as the Ghost Dance adherents explained it. McLaughlin wrote that the Lakota were "excited" over a "return of the ghosts," when white men would be annihilated and Indian lands and life restored. McLaughlin wrote that the Lakota had learned that the Great Spirit had sent the Europeans to punish them for their sins, and that their purgatory was now over, and spring would be the time of deliverance. All the lost people, buffalo, game, and the land itself would be restored. These spirits were already gathering at the boundaries of the Spirit World and crossing into the earth-plane, driving before them immense herds of buffalo and beautiful, fine horses as gifts for the living.

> "The Great Spirit, who had so long deserted his red children, was now once more with them and against the whites, and the white man's gunpowder would no longer have the power to drive a bullet through the skin of an Indian. The whites themselves would soon be overwhelmed and smothered under a deep land-

slide, held down by sod and timber, and the few who might escape would become small fishes in the rivers. In order to bring about this happy result, the Indians must believe and organize the Ghost Dance. . . ." (MOONEY, 1892)

The Lakota believed that the landslide would be accompanied by whirlwinds and floods; floodwaters would rise up and flow into the mouths of the whites and choke them with mud. The Lakota would rise above these floods and ride the whirlwinds, with the feathers of the crow in their hair. Lakota were encouraged to put away anything related to the white world, to dress in buckskins and white shirts, called "ghost shirts," and to dance and wait for deliverance. Among the Lakota, all dancers wore this "ghost shirt," men, women, and children; some believed that the shirts were bulletproof and magically protected the wearer. The shirts were occasionally simple and unadorned, but most incorporated paintings or beadwork representations of the sun, moon, stars, crow, magpie, and eagle. Sometimes the fringes were painted with red ochre, the sacred color of Wovoka. Eagle feathers were attached to the garment, and crow feathers were twisted into the dancers' hair.

What is remembered by the United States as the closing chapter in the Indian wars occurred soon after Chief Sitting Bull's death on December 15, 1890, at Standing Rock by Lakota police. The murder of more than three hundred unarmed Lakota men, women, and children took place on December 29, 1890, where they had gathered at Wounded

Knee on the Pine Ridge Agency to dance the Ghost Dance.
Members of the United States Cavalry—the "Black Ninth,"
the First, and the Sixth—went to the Indians' camp to stop
the dancing. Representatives of the ranking chief, Big Foot,
met them and explained that the group was friendly, that they
were only praying, and that they would obey any orders the
soldiers gave them. Big Foot even placed a white flag in his
camp as a mark of peace. The chief himself was in his tipi,
sick with pneumonia.

Despite the Indians' efforts, the soldiers attempted to stop
the ceremonies. During a round-up of dancers, a medicine
man named Yellow Bird encouraged the warriors to resist;
these men were armed with knives and clubs, not guns. Pre-
dictably, scuffles broke out, and the hostilities quickly escalated.
The soldiers turned Hotchkiss guns on fleeing children and
pursued mothers with infants at their breasts, turning resistance into an orgy of blood. For days after the murders,
the soldiers dumped the bodies of their victims in a mass
trench-grave at the killing field. (Red paint was used in the
Ghost Dance as a sign of rebirth; to this day, red paint and
red banners can be seen along the trenchline, put there by
relatives of the Indian people who died in the massacre.)

In later interviews about Lakota interpretations of his
doctrine, Wovoka disclaimed all responsibility and stressed
his message of universal peace. He said that the Lakota had
brought destruction on themselves by ignoring his words not
to fight and to always do good to both red and white.

Whites interpreted the Ghost Dance as a desperate

reaction of conquered peoples to insurmountable odds. They dismissed it as tragic and ill-fated, and some said it "helped prepare the tribes for Christianity." But the Father's Dance, brought to the tribes by Wovoka, was far more than a reaction. It was a prayer for survival and strength to endure the unendurable. Whites were slaughtering millions of game animals, including the buffalo on the Great Plains. Their thirst for gold and other minerals tore into the Earth herself, destroying the land. Canadians and Americans imposed alien reservation systems on the tribes and wrested the land from those who had always lived upon it.

The tribes saw what was happening to the land and its denizens, and they knew that they and their children were the victims of the invaders. Whites predicted the complete elimination of Indian cultures at this time, and their governments ordered people like Mooney to document these last days because they didn't think native peoples would survive. While the Father's Dance was in part a prayer to end the madness, it was first and foremost a prayer for survival.

Land, religion, and identity are inextricable in the indigenous world, and Wovoka's dance provided hope. Today, it is possible to believe that Crow heard the prayers and saw the suffering. The buffalo have come back, as have the elk and deer. The people have survived. Native populations have recovered to pre-Columbian levels (about three million), and people pray the old prayers and teach their children the right ways to live. Crow Woman's voice calls out to us across time and space from the dance circle:

The crow—Ehe'eye!
The crow—Ehe'eye!
I saw him when he flew down,
I saw him when he flew down.
To the earth,
To the earth.
He has renewed our life,
He has renewed our life.
He has taken pity on us,
He has taken pity on us.

Raven, Crow,
and Edgar Allan Poe

*E*uropeans were Christianized by the time they stumbled upon the shores of the New World. A thousand years of Judeo-Christian heritage and Islamic influence changed old European concepts of animism and Nature worship; they did not view the world and all of its creatures as sacred, as once had their ancestors. By the time Europeans came into Raven's American world, Nature was considered an adversary to be conquered, a dark, threatening force that tested human mettle. They no longer viewed themselves as part of Nature—they thought themselves separate and alone.

Subsequent contacts with indigenous religions and their exposure to the wild land, a land they intended to domesticate, shaped American values, whether they realized it or not, and molded these children of European immigrants into something new. The American experience in the Great Wilderness was forever engraved into the national psyche. It brought these descendants of people who had long before danced to the drum-beats of the Great Goddess and lived by the rhythms of the seasons back into contact with what they had forgotten.

Celtic Europeans had once viewed Raven as a manifestation of the Earth Mother and honored her as Bodh, Great Raven of Battle, in her fiercely protective form. Other Europeans, even after coming to the New World, affiliated Raven with magic and healing. The formal religions of Europe may have ignored basic components of the old religions, but many forms and functions of these beliefs survived in the folklore the immigrants brought with them. Europeans and their American descendants viewed ravens and crows with a mixture of respect and suspicion.

Europeans associated ravens and crows with darkness and death. Observed feeding on the carrion of battlefields and attacking the crops, the birds were viewed as agents of destruction. They did, however, retain their allegorical roles as intermediaries between the living and the spirit worlds, as is clearly illustrated in Edgar Allan Poe's masterpiece, *The Raven.* No compendium considering raven and crow in North America can ignore Poe's raven. In the poem, the bird comes as a messenger to a man who lost his lady-love to the arms of Death.

Poe, one of the greatest American writers of the nineteenth century, lived from 1809-1849. The son of itinerant actors, orphaned at an early age, Poe worked as a journalist, editor, and writer; he profited little from his books. Although he was the recipient of limited literary acclaim from the East Coast intellectual establishment, his unconventional beliefs and habits did not fit well within mainstream literary circles. He was fascinated by the occult, by the mysteries and terrors of death, and the possibility of life after death. This spiritual and intellectual thirst was matched, if not overcome, by a thirst for alcohol and addictions to whiskey and opium.

Treasures of American literature, Poe's works dealt with life and death, love and hate, justice and vengeance, the divinity of Nature, and the mysteries of eternities beyond life. Dying a pauper in Baltimore in 1849, Poe influenced generations of writers; entire schools of writing and philosophy have emulated his work in Europe.

A contemporary of Washington Irving and James Fenimore Cooper (whose work brought them money and fame), Poe was part of the American Romantic movement. The vast wildness of the American continent made its imprint on the American Romantics, nurturing their love of Nature and their respect and adulation of the American Indian as "The Noble Savage." Poe's voice — seeker of truth and delver in black mysteries — exposed the darker side of the emerging American psyche. Wrestling with the inevitability of death and desperate hope for rebirth in a new life, what better emissary than the raven could Poe have imagined?

Poe clearly understood ambivalent Euro-American attitudes towards ravens, but he also understood the birds' innate intelligence and dignity. When Poe wrote, "Open here I flung the shutter, when, with many a flirt and flutter / In there stepped a stately Raven of the saintly days of yore. / Not the least obeisance made he; / not a minute stopped or stayed he; / But, with mien of lord or lady, perched above my chamber door. / Perched upon a bust of Pallas just above my chamber door. / Perched, and sat, and nothing more," he was clearly establishing the bird's nobility. By having the raven perch on top of a replica of Pallas (Pallas Athena), he associated it with knowledge and wisdom, for Athena is the Greek goddess of wisdom, a Hellenized version of a very ancient Great Goddess. In Poe's poem, the raven is her familiar and emissary, sent to a distraught lover to tell him that, separated by death from Lenore, the only way the two would be reunited was *through* death. The raven offered no cure for the man's emotional and physical suffering, he offered no panacea when the sufferer asked, "Tell me . . . is there balm in Gilead?" All he said was "Nevermore."

Many Americans view Poe's raven as a portent of dread, an emissary of evil. But it is doubtful that was Poe's intent. It has been noted that in conversations with his contemporaries, Poe said that he had originally wanted to use a parrot as the messenger from the spirit world because he was impressed with the vocalizations and mimicry of human speech of a family parrot. But, Poe said, after watching the comic antics of parrots, he knew that no parrot could inspire foreboding, so he chose the raven, and in so doing, reinforced Euro-American perceptions about the bird.

Poe lived during a time when America's Indian wars were raging, but the final resolution was clear. He lived in an era of slavery, of brewing civil war, of the fulfillment of Manifest

Destiny and the building of railroads across the continent.
Poe's dark mysticism and the birth of the American Romantic
Movement, shaped by the expansion of the American land-
base and its contacts with indigenous peoples, continue in
some ways to influence American thought and religion. Once
the continent was conquered by Euro-Americans and Euro-
Canadians, the land and its peoples asserted their slow and
subtle influences. First, the mainstream culture sought to turn
the continent into an agricultural center, then, with the advent
of the American Industrial Revolution, factories, complete
with coal mines, dams, and uranium pits, were the driving force.
By the turn of the twentieth century, old Judeo-Christian and
Puritanical ways of thinking were challenged by people like
Aleister Crowley (who urged a return to paganism and is, in
fact, one of the founding fathers of what is termed Wicca, a
rediscovery of paganism and "New Age" religions); Isadora
Duncan, the dancer who sought to integrate Nature-worship
into her choreography; and other American Neo-Classicists.

Two world wars and several generations later, following in
the footsteps of Poe, Crowley, and Duncan, the beatniks of
the fifties and early sixties, and hippies of the sixties' American
Renaissance rejected the legacy of environmental destruction,
racism, and materialism. They turned to the indigenous
Americans and their religions for guidance; they turned inward,
to Hindu, Taoist, Buddhist, and shamanic philosophies. This
movement has accelerated over the last three decades and is
currently in lively flower; large, sophisticated, and active groups
such as Greenpeace and the Sierra Club exercise considerable

political clout, and hundreds of smaller organizations work for the preservation of specific causes. Interest in Wicca and other so-called pagan religions is also on the rise. The environmentalists and nature religionists may well be the world's last Ghost Dancers.

SCIENCE AND LAW

A Separate World

he study, regulation, and protection of ravens and crows reflect human curiosity and concern about other creatures who inhabit the planet. Science and law are a far cry from the mystic expressed in creation stories, or danced on the Plains, or explored by writers such as Poe, but the work done in these areas provides yet another dimension to the understanding of the raven and the crow.

Who are they, these dark entities that have inspired such reverence, awe, and joy in human beings? In scientific terms, both belong to the same genus *Corvus* (plural, *Corvidae*). Americans tend to think of ravens as large black birds that make squawking, croaking sounds, and the crow as a smaller version; they often confuse the two. When James Mooney wrote, "The raven, which is practically a larger crow and which lives in the mountains, but occasionally comes down into the plains, is also held sacred and regarded as a bringer of omens by the Prairie tribes, as well as by the Tlinkit and others of the northwest coast and by the Cherokee in the east," he was reflecting a popular and commonsense understanding. There are, however, differences between members of the genus Corvus.

There are forty-one species of crows* world-wide. In North America, *Corvus corax* is the Common Raven, and *Corvus brachyrhynchos* is the American Crow. Other members of the raven and crow family include the jays, magpies, and nutcrackers. Corvidae are omnivorous and opportunistic; they eat meat and plant foods, and have generally done well within human populations in North America. Crows are part of the Order *Passeriformes,* which includes songbirds; raven and crow are the group's largest members, though not everyone finds their songs particularly melodious. They have intelligence and the companion of intelligence, humour.

Ravens are physically larger than crows. Their wingspan can measure over four feet, and their tail is blunt and wedge-shaped, a feature most easily seen when the raven is in flight. A raven's beak is very prominent with a distinctive, aquiline shape. Both ravens and crows are capable of an amazing range of sounds, but the raven's vocalizations are usually deeper than those of the crow. While ornithologists call the raven the "genius of the bird world," crows and the other corvids are not far behind in intelligence.

Ravens are amazingly beautiful and graceful flyers, maneuvering effortlessly in the sky, whirling and twirling and gliding through the air, riding the updrafts and the wind with ease. Sometimes, the whoosh-whoosh sound of a raven on the wing

---

*In this section, when the word "crow" is used, it is intended to encompass both crows and ravens, unless otherwise specified.

can be heard in the forest (a sound I have only heard from ravens in flight). Some ornithologists say this is more than the friction of the wind against the wind—that the raven deliberately makes this sound to announce his presence.

The American crow is smaller and can be recognized by its voice and squared tail. The crow's beak is more narrow and pointed than a raven's, without the raven's characteristic hooked shape. Both crow and raven beaks are met by a deli-

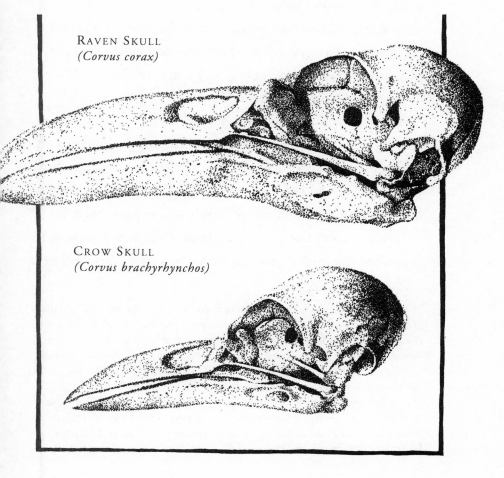

RAVEN SKULL
(Corvus corax)

CROW SKULL
(Corvus brachyrhynchos)

cate matting of fine feathers and nasal bristles. Scientists say that the color of the birds' sleek, black feathers was naturally selected for survival reasons, to make corvids conspicuous during the day. Birds that are easily recognized by their fellows are more successful in social interaction, courtship, and territorial defense. Black helps birds be inconspicuous at night, when predators such as owls hunt; it also blends in with forest shade, protecting them when they take their daily naps. The mirrorlike specular reflections, which give crows and ravens their shiny, rainbow-like appearance in the sunlight, depend on strong angular reflection.* This reflection, when the light plays on the bird's body exactly right, also creates the illusion of the white crow or white raven.

Corvids have elaborate languages and they are also expert mimics. A local crow developed an entire routine of barks imitating neighborhood dogs; he barked like the dog next door, imitated the sound of barks from a long distance, whimpered like a small puppy, and whined like a dog begging for food. **

Raven vocalizations are much more than music, although some find the birds' voices far from pleasing to the ear. But to

---

*I first studied ravens with an Absorka friend in Yellowstone Park. We discovered a raven who frequented the area around a small and beautiful geyser pool. Sometimes, the spray from the geyser misted his feathers, and when he flew across the clearing, little droplets of moisture metamorphosed into diamonds and rubies on the raven's wings. We called him "The Wizard" and spent hours with him in the geyser clearing.

**One February afternoon, while walking through a pine grove, I stopped to listen to a raven repertoire of whistles, squeaks, and chirps. When a train whistle sounded in the distance, the bird became silent, but within a few seconds, a cacophony of "Whoo— ooooh—ooh," resounded through the trees.

those who love ravens, their voices are beautiful. Ravensong indicates many things: where the nearest food is, what animals and birds are in the neighborhood, who is courting whom, whether or not something dangerous is near. In addition to their natural calls, corvids can also imitate other birds, falling water, and even the melody from a music box or tinkling ice-cream truck.*

Dr. Lawrence Kilham, author of *On Watching Birds* (winner of the John Burroughs Medal for nature-writing) and *The American Crow and Common Raven*, is America's foremost expert on crows and ravens. He and his wife Jane have spent decades with them; he maintains that only by listening, watching, and spending time with corvids can one really begin to appreciate their vocalizations and the subtle ways in which they communicate. During the six years the Kilhams spent on a Florida ranch observing wild American crows, they recorded calls and studied daily crow activities. Dr. Kilham has hand-raised crows and ravens, and currently his family maintains a small rehabilitation center at their New Hampshire home. He has spent hours in cold New England winters watching birds and has traversed the world in ornithological study. Despite a lifetime of bird-watching and a close relationship with the corvid family, he says it is only now, as he enters his eightieth decade, that he is beginning to understand them. Much of

---

* A crow I rehabilitated enjoyed music-box tunes. His favorite was the Neapolitan classic, *Torno a Sorrento*, and he sang his own peculiarly corvid interpretation of the music on occasion.

what is known about crow and raven family life is the direct result of Kilham's work.

Studying the birds presents many challenges—for one, it can be difficult to tell individuals apart until the observer has spent time with them and learned to recognize distinguishing characteristics. Also, it is difficult to tell the sex of crows without direct observation of mating or DNA testing. "I must admit that when I started watching corvids, much of what I saw was confusing," Kilham wrote. "In studying woodpeckers I was usually watching a single pair, with the sexes differing in plumage. With the crows in Florida, I found myself looking at a group of individuals that looked much alike. A few discoveries, however, provided ways of organizing. One was that a cattle drive (a track bordered on either side by wire fences) was a territorial boundary between two groups of seven to nine crows. A second discovery, following shortly thereafter, was that each group consisted of a breeding pair plus auxiliaries. I was to find out that the latter aided in all phases of nesting. It was exciting to discover that crows were cooperative breeders. I could not find a single paper on the cooperative breeding of American Crows in the literature, nor any on their territorial behavior. I was to learn in the next year or two that many aspects of crow behavior had either never been reported or were mentioned only in minimal detail by others." (KILHAM, 1989)

Since the release of Kilham's corvid research, a number of amateur birdwatchers and graduate students have shared their observations about crows and ravens with him, further reinforcing what he discovered. Crows live in family groups; others, often their own offspring, aid in the nesting and feeding of the chicks and in defending group territories. Family life is the core of corvid existence.

Crows usually mate for life. They develop tightly knit family groups and each group establishes, maintains, and defends its own territory. They are cooperative breeders; the chicks of previous seasons grow into adolescence and remain with the parents rather than leave within a few months of hatching to form their own nesting units. They help raise the new season's simps (juveniles), and may spend two to three seasons with their parents before they embark on their own nesting. Since corvids can live for twenty years, it appears that they learn from their parents and other crows the skills necessary for survival.

When asked how crows and ravens see the world, Kilham said, "Well, I think one thing they see, as the crows are cooperative breeders, are those of their own group—others that they recognize individually. I think that is one of the things that means a lot to them. And then they keep a sharp eye out for any kind of trespassers. Down there in Florida, they would pay no attention to the crows of other groups until one of those crows came to the borderline [of the group's territory] and immediately they'd go there. They may scatter to go foraging and if one finds something interesting, then they all fly over there to see what it is. If that happens to be something like a frog, the [one] that found it will keep it, and they will all stand around and look at the crow with the frog; it may look like they will attack and try and take it from him, but they never do. The thing is, they respect one who has found food—the attitude seems to be 'finders keepers,' even if you are one of the lowest members of the hierarchy, what you find is yours; they don't rob each other. If these types of behavior were exhibited, it would break up the whole group. If the individual that caught something wasn't allowed to keep it and was robbed, I think that the cooperative spirit would fall apart.

"I remember the time when I saw a couple of crows find a diamondback rattler. The other crows saw there was something over there and they all flew over and followed the rattlesnake, walking along behind him. But then, after a while, it didn't interest them. They couldn't kill it, and they didn't regard it as dangerous and so they all just flew off. Finally, [I feel that] when a crow looks out at the world, the first thing it sees is the family circle, its mate, their chicks, its family. The birds look at the world in terms of taking care of these family members and themselves."

Crows and ravens are notorious nest-looters; they will eat eggs and even nestlings of other birds. They also hunt mice, small reptiles, and other animals. They will fly above a mouse nest, wait for a mouse to come out, then dive down and sink their bill deep into the hapless creature. They have been known to shake palmetto palm trees, loosening edible vermin, lizards, and small snakes from their hiding places in order to eat them. Given the opportunity, like hawks, eagles, and vultures, they will eat carrion, too. During courtship, the birds seek out all types of food to bring to each other—after all, one must be a good provider to take care of a family.

Corvid families and territorial groups are gregarious and

sociable. They want to "flock," to belong to a group. The birds accrue many benefits by belonging: living cooperatively can ensure safety and sufficient food. Sometimes, when separated from their families or territorial groups, the lone corvid tries to become a member of another flock.

One way that a lone crow can gain acceptance into a territorial group is by helping nesting females, sharing food, and working to make itself indispensable to the group. Sometimes dominant males accept the loner and permit its incorporation, and sometimes the loner is driven off. Rejected by one territorial group, it may be accepted by another.

Baby crows are called simps, and when a simp hatches, it has a lot to learn in order to survive. Like other intelligent animals, simps learn how to live and communicate from their parents and other members of the cooperative unit. They learn to hunt, forage, and survive from these family groups.

Unlike many other birds, when young crows fledge, they do not necessarily leave the nest and their parents permanently. Family units, with the breeding pair, may be accompanied by juveniles who serve as helpers to their parents for up to two years. During this time, the young birds learn important survival details—the dangers of predators, details of hunting and scavenging, and aspects of crow social interaction.

Family and cooperative breeding groups can number up to nine individuals. Corvids would not be as successful if they did not live in these groups. Family helpers—avian babysitters—allow parents to devote more time to tasks such as female incubating, brooding, cleaning parasites out of the nests, and guarding the nest during incubation, keeping predators away. Logical benefits accrue from cooperation—if a parent dies, the surviving mate would be able to rear the young with the help of auxiliaries. Also, in a cooperative group, each nestling gets adequate attention, and in times when food is hard to find, more helpers mean more food.

"Having mature gonads does not mean that is ready to breed. It takes time for an intelligent and social animal, whether a crow or a primate, to learn the complex life of its species. Delayed breeding, with one to three or more years as members of a group, may be of value in providinging the time needed to reach a maturity that is more than physical." (KILHAM, 1989)

Crow territories are as large as ninety hectares (about 222 acres). Kilham's Florida crows lived on a remote ranch and were not afraid of people, because they had not been exposed to threatening humans. Corvids also exploit a wide range of environments, and urban populations are on the upswing. From time to time, wandering flocks (of up to fifty members) with no clear territory of their own can be seen. It is likely that these are flocks of non-breeders, and it is not at all unusual to see flocks of juveniles living together in the fall and winter. They forage collectively, helping each other find food. (HEINRICH, 1989) It is possible that non-breeding crows and ravens flock until they go through courtship and mating phases and establish breeding pairs with helpers and territories of their own.

Crows

There are between two and twenty species of crows in North America—ornithologists disagree on the exact number—and all are long-lived; crows live about twenty years, and have lived longer in captivity as pets. *Corvus ossifrugas,* commonly called the "fish crow," is a small crow that lives in coastal areas from New England down the Atlantic coast and into eastern Texas, in tidewater areas and river valleys. While gregarious with their own kind, fish crows are nefarious predators of sea birds and their young. This makes them unpopular in some human circles.

The crow Americans are most likely to encounter is *C. brachyrhynchus,* the American crow. The birds have expanded their niches, and as human populations have grown larger in North America, so have their numbers. They are amazingly prolific and adaptable. However, in the state of Hawaii, the status of the American crow's cousin, *C. tropicus,* is not as happy. Apparently due to the tremendous influx of humans to the islands in this century and resultant damage to Hawaiian crow forest environments and nesting areas, this little crow species is on the edge of extinction.

The American crow can be divided into four subspecies: Eastern, Southern, Florida, and Western. The birds show only slight differences in their sizes, appearing essentially the same otherwise.

An adult crow will measure seventeen to twenty-one inches in length. There is no sexual dimorphism in crows—males and females look alike, at least to us. Today, the gender of a crow, like other hard-to-sex birds, can be learned through a blood test in which DNA is analyzed. This is a great improvement over past years, when sexing was done surgically, with a small incision made to see if the bird had ovaries or testicles.

Simps and the Beginning Days

When crow simps hatch, they are not beautiful. Tiny, naked, ugly little chicks, with blotchy black-and- brown skin, they gradually get their pinfeathers and become more presentable; in their early days, only their mother could love them. The finest description of a simp I have ever read was written by an amateur ornithologist: "He was about three weeks old and the ugliest of babies, with a livid brown and bluish-black skin, half-hidden by rough, black pinfeathers, and an enormous stomach. His legs and feet were far too big for him. He had a huge wobbly head on a skinny neck, [and] a gaping bright red, velvet mouth constantly open for food. . . ." (BYERS, 1990)

Crow parents and their helpers are kept constantly busy feeding their two to five hatchlings. Generally, the mother stays close to the nest, the father keeps a wary eye out for intruders and predators, and the helpers feed the simps, clean fecal sacs out of the nest, repair nest damage, assist as look-outs, and other parental duties. During brooding, the helpers will feed the mother while the father posts a wary guard over the nest.

Within three weeks of hatching, simps begin to feather out and start to look more like birds and less like aliens from outer space. Transforming from hatchlings to fledglings, within five or six weeks they are fully feathered. They begin stretching and flapping their wings in preparation for the flying life.

Simps are always hungry, and they enhance their vulnerability to predators by their repeated cries for food. When anything flutters by their nest, they lean their little heads back, and their red mouths gape. (Young crows continue to have red-and-pinkish gapes for the first year of life.) When simps become frightened and if a parent or helper is present or nearby, they panic and cry piteously. If there are no obvious protectors conveniently close, they prudently remain silent. However, simps are rarely left alone for long periods, due to the vigilance of their family groups.

By six to eight weeks, simps learn to fly, albeit awkwardly at first. Sometimes, the skill is rudely thrust upon a fledgling; blown from the nest, or falling out and in a panic, a fledgling will usually discover its amazing ability.

It takes two to three years for young crows to learn all they need to know about independent living. As has been mentioned, they will frequently spend several nesting seasons with the family group. Finally, they are fully imprinted and enculturated as crows.

Imprinting and Socialization

Corvid imprinting is somewhat different than the imprinting of ducks and geese, as explained by the ethologist Konrad Z. Lorenz, who raised goslings at his Altenberg home. Goslings commonly imprint upon the first moving, animate thing they see, and these goslings imprinted on Lorenz shortly after they hatched. They saw him as their "mother," and followed him devotedly. Lorenz studied their calls and learned to communicate like a goose with them.

Corvid imprinting is more complicated. They are enculturated as crows and ravens, and they imprint upon the family unit over an extended period of time. They can, however, become part of a human social family unit if taken into a family at the fledgling stage. "Ducks are very different from passerine birds," Dr. Kilham explained during a discussion on corvid imprinting. "When they hatch, [within] a very short time they become imprinted. Whereas with crows and ravens, they imprint over a fairly long stretch of weeks. So even though the crow is already out of the nest, he still can imprint on people. . . . When we had crows here, for example, in Lyme, they imprinted on us and recognized our family; the same thing [was true of] crows we raised in Bethesda, Maryland. They knew us as a family, but if any strange boy came into our yard to play, they'd attack him. So they imprinted on [us particularly, not humans in general]; we were, what I think in Nature would have been their own group. All of my family belonged to their circle."

The need for belonging and the identification with family
and group are important for crows and ravens, particularly in
the development of identity and survival skills. A local woman
found a young crow, not more than six months old, that had
obviously become separated from its family; it had been standing at a particular spot on the roadside for five days. When
she realized something was seriously wrong, she stopped and
captured the bird and brought it to her home, where she kept
it in the garage and fed it dogfood, bread, and water until she
could locate someone to care for it.

There had been hailstorms the week before the finding of
the juvenile, and when it was brought to the author, it was
carefully examined for any signs of damage; hailstorms injure
(or kill) many birds. No clear signs of head or brain damage
were found, but the bird was extremely docile, perhaps more
from hunger and exposure than anything else. Taken to the
veterinarian for a second examination, a possible head injury
was the diagnosis. It was later learned through an x-ray that
the bird had been shot, and a pellet was lodged in her wing.
The exterior wound had healed, but much rehabilitation
work remained.

Gradually, the bird regained its strength and became interested in a more "normal" crow life. Today, she flies and cautious-
ly interacts with other birds; however, she is still afraid of
other crows, and has much to learn in terms of lifeskills. In
many ways, she seems confused about what to do in the wild.

In the case of a little one-winged yearling rehabilitated at
the Icarus Facility in Verde Valley, Arizona (by one of the most

skilled of bird rehabilitators, Christy Van Cleeve), and christened "Tina" by staffers at the Window Rock Zoo, no return to normalcy was ever seen. Tina, perhaps because of brain damage or a lack of socialization, did not vocalize with the other one-winged corvids at the zoo enclosure; she never hopped and climbed the trees in the enclosure or played with Big Raven and Gagee, a raven and crow who also reside there. She remained silent and spent her days walking along the bottom of the enclosure. She lived in Window Rock from September until February, and then died. Perhaps she was more damaged than rehabilitators realized, or perhaps an interrupted socialization process indirectly led to her demise. One can only speculate as to the reasons, but perhaps, like feral children raised by animals and then reintroduced to human society, corvids who "do not belong," whether to a human or a bird family group, do not do well in life.

Courtship and Nest-building

When all goes well in a crow's life, it will enter into the rituals of nest-building after three years of learning social, communication, and survival skills. Courtship begins in early spring, usually February or March. This is the time when so-called "murders" of crows (groups of more than ten individuals) begin to show off for each other, with suitors whirling through the air, trying to impress the chosen one. Chirps and gurgles echo through the trees, and crows bring each other special, delectable treats. In time, murders break down into pairs, and soon, nest-building begins.

Crows are very cagey about their nesting sites; they want
to keep them secret from predators, and they consider humans
to be potential predators. It is usually difficult to locate a nest,
particularly during courtship and nest-building time.

Crows like their nests high above the ground, twenty-five
to seventy feet in the air. They prefer trees, but are so adaptable
that they have learned to utilize cliffs, rock crevices, and even
church steeples and belfreys. Sometimes, they will build their
nests on the crown of a tree; evergreens are favorite sites. They
prefer easy access to water and to food, so if there are ponds
or lakes surrounded by trees that shelter ducks, geese, grebes,
and red-winged blackbirds, crows are likely to nest nearby.

A crow nest comprises three parts—a base foundation, a
bowl, and a cup (the inside of the nest). Made of small sticks,
a quarter to a half-inch thick and ten to eighteen inches long,
the nest's base is usually twenty-two to twenty-eight inches
wide, the bowl is about a foot wide, and the cup about nine
inches deep. Crows gather and shred all types of materials—
bark, rags, wool, animal fur, human hair, yarn, ribbons, feathers, moss—for a soft, warm lining. It takes about two weeks
for crows to build a new nest, while nest-improvement time
depends upon the amount of work needed to make the old
nest cozy.

Crows return to the same nests each season. Parents and
their juvenile helpers will work together getting the nest ready
for the eggs. Crows generally build and repair nests early in
the day; by noon, they become hungry and after they eat, will
generally take a nap until mid-afternoon.

Egg-laying, -brooding, and -hatching occurs at various times in spring throughout North America, depending upon climate and elevation. During brooding, the female generally does not leave the nest; the male or the helpers will feed the female.

The extended crow family provides for and protects the simp, but despite the most diligent care, it is not uncommon for one or two to fall out of the nest and die. Accidents, predators (especially humans), hailstorms, or strong winds can decimate a family unit. Sometimes, competitive nestmates will eject weak or late-hatchlings in the scuffle for food. Life in the wild is precarious: ornithologists estimate that over fifty percent of simps do not survive their first year of life.

Crow Diseases

Veterinarians and ornithologists point out that crows, like other corvids, are very resistant to infections and many of the diseases that plague other passerines. They also admit that not much is known about what diseases *do* affect them. Things happen quickly in the wild world. If a bird is injured or becomes sick, it either recovers quickly and lives, or succumbs and dies.

Crows and Water

Like other birds, crows are attracted by water. Regardless of weather or temperature, they will bathe every day if given the opportunity. Crows have been observed splashing in melted snowbanks, in small puddles, and in the shallows of lakes. If there is no melted water available, crows will dive headfirst

into snowbanks and take snow baths. Afterward, crows preen
themselves, cleaning and adjusting every feather.

Mobbing Behaviors

Because they are intelligent, crows are wary and alert and
look out after each other. Crows defend their own territories,
but have also been seen to come to the assistance of crows
outside of their family circle, mob intruders, and then "police"
the area where the mobbing occurred to prevent the intruders'
return. Crows have a distress call and this attracts other crows
to the area to help them.

In one instance, a cat walked along an area where crows
were feeding and bathing beside a stream. The alert was
sounded, and within minutes, dozens of crows (and even a
few ravens) flew into the area, taking up the call and flying
low over the cat. The cat was dive-bombed a couple of times
and then retreated—running away from the stream-forest
interface and back toward the houses of men. In a matter of
minutes, the cat was nowhere to be seen. However, raucous
callings and reconnaissance flights continued in the area for
another two hours. Finally, the murder dispersed and life
returned to normal along the river bank.

On another occasion, early one January, a young golden
eagle flew into crow territory in a woods behind a motel. It
roosted on an old snag, but the snag was in the territory of a
crow clan and they didn't want the eagle around. The alarm
was sounded, and the crow clan gathered. Crows from outside the clan territory came too, and singly as well as two-by-

two, the crows flew close to the golden one, cawing and threatening the eagle. After about half an hour of this unsolicited attention, the eagle flew south, across the road and away from the mobbing. The eagle had not displayed any interest in the crows, or foraged while in their territory, but that didn't seem to make any difference.

Some have described highly organized groups of crows and gatherings of crow clans on neutral territory to enforce what seemed to be crow "codes of conduct." People have told stories of crow funerals, and the phenomenon of the "King Crow," a dominant male among dominant males, is sometimes mentioned. There is so much crow lore that it can be difficult to sort out corvid fact from human fantasy. However, a great deal of complicated social interaction can be documented—crows surrounding injured clan members to protect them from intruders and murmuring mournful cries when a family member has been badly injured—so the idea of a "King Crow" is not totally preposterous.

Roosting

Crows only live in nests when they are young and when they are brooding. During the rest of the year, they sleep in favorite roosting spots. In the mountains and forests surrounding Flagstaff, Arizona, different families have specific roosting areas. In other regions, crows sometimes roost together in groups numbering in the hundreds. When the sun sets, crows become extremely drowsy, and enter into a deep sleep. They are most vulnerable to attack at night.

A Day in the Life of a Crow

A crow's day begins at sunrise. After awakening, he flies from his roost to a nearby water source to drink and bathe. The crow will then preen himself and set his feathers gently in place, then commute to his day territory to forage; this territory can be as far away as forty miles from the roosting site or very close to the roost and the water source.

Crows are omnivorous. During spring and summer, they will waddle on the ground, working parks, golf courses, and other open, grassy areas in their hunt for juicy worms. They search for worms much like a group of survey archaeologists, dividing up a grid area and scrounging. One by one, in a very determined manner, they scrupulously examine their particular patch of ground. In spring, they also watch for duck and goose eggs around ponds, lakes, and wetlands.

Urban crows (and ravens) can be found around fast-food restaurants and grocery stores. Crows who work these territories regularly check out dumpsters and parking lots. University campuses, large lawns, and cemeteries are popular sources of worms and other foods as well. On campuses, crows feast from dining room dumpsters and enjoy the hustle and bustle of crowds moving from class to class.

Throughout the year, they take advantage of whatever carrion they can find. During summer and fall, crows feed primarily on seeds and various plants. In winter, they enjoy the suet concerned humans put outside for local birds.

After feeding throughout the morning, crows take a nap. In summer, they will fly into nearby woods to rest in the cool shadows of sheltering trees. During the winter, they often find sunny places to roost and relax. By mid-afternoon, regardless of the season, they become active again and prepare for the commute back to the night-roosting place. They will forage again, drink, and bathe, and then return to the roost. They seem to try to be back well before sundown to secure just the right sleeping spot.

Crow Affection and Bonding

Even as simps, crows develop strong attachments to their families, both biological and surrogate, if they are being hand-raised by humans. They are very aware of the world around them, and of other entities inhabiting that world. Each individual has a different personality, and they develop ties and friendships with all types of creatures.

In nature, simps bond with siblings, their parents, and auxiliaries. Crow mates show affection for one another, both in and out of courtship season. They protect and defend each other, and seem to grieve when a member of the group is hurt or dies. In the case of one crow found and rehabilitated by the author, his family surrounded him, calling, obviously worried. During his recovery, his relatives and corvid friends came to his aviary and visited with him. They cawed to each other, and he shovelled food out to them. In winter, he even shared food with the local chickadees.

At one point, there were two injured crows in the author's backyard aviary. The older crow took a parental interest in a little fledgling whose right leg had been badly crushed as a result of a fall. The young one, Wimi, seemed to look to the older one, Gagee, as a role model, and Gagee seemed to enjoy caring for the little one. He fed the young crow bread and other foods, and looked after him. The little bird never fully recovered, despite the best of nutrition and veterinary care, and one night during a tremendous thunderstorm, his heart stopped and he died. Gagee didn't vocalize for four days.

Naturalists say that fear of thunder and hailstorms is common in crows and ravens. During thunderstorms, groups of ravens have been observed huddled together in low-lying tree branches, close to the trunks, crying piteously, heads shaking with fear; "heart attacks" have been known to occur at these times. Wimi was never a strong or healthy simp and even though he and Gagee were secure and protected and their aviary covered during the storm, it proved to be too much for the little one. The storm that came down from the mountains Navajos call "Where the Thunder Sleeps," outside of Flagstaff, Arizona, was quite spectacular and frightening. Sheets of water and tongues of flame shot through the skies, and bolts of lightning flashed and thunder shook the ground throughout the night.*

In the case of hand-raised crows, crows raised by human beings, bonding occurs, as mentioned earlier. Simps bond to

---

*I like to think that *Angwusi Navoti* (Crow Mother), Mother of All the Kachinas, came down to Flagstaff with her sons and the Cloud People that night to take Wimi home, where he was made whole and complete and free from pain. We buried him on the slopes of the San Francisco Peaks, not far from an ancient Hopi water shrine; the base of these mountains was once the home of the Hopi Crow Clan, which eventually became known as the Kachina Clan. Perhaps Wimi is now a crow kachina.

their human families and have even been known to bond with family dogs, whose tails they tug in play, or in many instances, in an attempt to get the dog to drop food. This not only displays humor, but is also a clever ploy to steal food.

Crows, coyotes, and wolves have been known to develop unique symbiotic relationships. Navajos, Hopis, Koyukon, and other indigenous American peoples say that crows and these members of the dog family help each other hunt. Crows and ravens have been observed to lead coyotes and wolves to prey, and then share in the meat.

Crow Memory

Crows remember things, events, and people very well, especially things that have either frightened or delighted them. They also seem to be fast learners. Dr. Loline Hathaway, curator of the Navajo Nation Zoological and Botanical Park, was part of a family who raised pecans. She once said that one of the biggest mistakes she ever made was a futile attempt to stop crows looting the family orchards. Crows love nuts, and were enjoying dining on them. Trying to frighten the cagey crows away from the nuts was ineffective, so one day, she got her shotgun and went out and shot at the birds.

"I was wearing a turquoise blue shirt that day," Dr. Hathaway recalled. "Well, some time after that, my sister went into the pecan grove wearing a blue shirt. She was mobbed by angry crows. The shooting didn't stop them, it just made them angry."

Crows also remember things and events that make them happy. When Dr. Kilham studied crows, he would fill his pockets with dried corn and distribute this corn to the crows as he walked along. One day he forgot to bring the corn, much to the disappointment of the eager crows. He looked back, and noticed the crows making demanding pecking motions—a pantomime of eating corn—on the ground, to communicate their desire.

Crows may or may not speak and understand human words, but they certainly know how to make known their desires to human beings. The author's crow friend, Gagee, never hesitated to let her know when he was out of food in his aviary. He would catch her eye through the sliding glass door that separated the study from his garden house and if he was out of puppy chow, would pantomime eating, repeating his display until the appropriate food was delivered to him.

Food Storing

Whenever crows gain access to more food than they can eat at one time, they will find a place to hide and store (cache) it. They have been known to hide food in tree crevices or dig a storage hole in the ground, placing their food in it and covering it with leaves. They remember where they cache food and return to it in times of need. Crows sometimes spy on ravens to see where they cache their food, and will rob the ravens. Ravens will also rob crow caches; spectacular aerial battles ensue when crows and ravens discover each other looting caches. Crows have been observed to hide favorite playthings like bottle tops, colored pieces of glass, and bits of metal.

Allopreening

Paired crows (as well as ravens) will tenderly stoke the feathers, head, and eye area of one another in a behavior called allopreening. This serves a purpose both of cleaning and of cementing affection and bonding. Males and females will allopreen each other, and will allopreen their simps as well.

Ravens

As might be expected since they are so closely related, crows and ravens share many traits and exhibit similar behaviors. The consensus among naturalists and ornithologists is that the raven is even brighter than his crow cousin, so some special aspects of raven behavior will be examined.

A well-known authority, Bernd Heinrich, has referred to ravens as "the *ne plus ultra* of up-and-coming birds." He wrote, "The corvid line (except for jays) radiated out [from forests] to occupy open land. Many of the more-recently evolved corvids now forage at least partially on the ground. Some have even adapted to treeless country and to nesting on cliffs. . . . Corvids [are]. . . large, intelligent, adaptable, ground-foraging birds independent of trees; it is probably only a slight exaggeration to say that the raven, *C. corax,* is the ultimate corvid. If so, it is also at the top of the most species-rich and rapidly evolving line of birds." (HEINRICH, 1989)

Individuals of the species vary in size, depending upon environment and genetic backgrounds. These birds can exploit a wide variety of climates and conditions, from the polar regions of the Arctic to the deserts, jungles, and mountains of North and Central America. The ancestral range of these giant crows included most of Europe, Asia, and North America. In modern times, much of their old forest range in southern Europe and the Mediterranean region has been decimated by human beings. Their numbers are growing in North America, however, despite human incursion.

In addition to its imposing size and impressive flying ability, the raven has a wide range of vocalizations. Its croaks and squawks are unmistakable, and when a raven imitates a human voice, the effect is uncanny.

Raven Family Life

Ravens live in family and clan territorial groups, spending years together. They mate for life, which may be as long as thirty years in the wild, and as long as sixty years in captivity. Like crows, a mated pair is sometimes accompanied by a third raven, who assists in daily family life.

Ravens court and mate in late winter or early spring, depending upon elevation and terrain. Their nests are found in cliffs and trees, although a local raven family selected the bell tower of a Catholic church for its nest site. Pairs frequently return to a previous year's nest, cleaning and rebuilding it for another year's use.

The family unit is the most important element in raven life. Mated pairs raise their chicks, and juveniles and adolescents stay with their parents for between two to three years to learn social and survival skills. It is not uncommon for juvenile

ravens to flock and assist each other in finding food, as
ornithologist Heinrich discovered and eloquently explained
in his book, *Ravens in Winter.* Heinrich was the first ornithologist to carefully study and document what he thought was
unusual behavior. One October day in 1984, Heinrich saw a
flock of ravens sharing their food and apparently calling other
ravens to come and eat with them. He studied raven behavior
for the next four years, and came to the conclusion that these
gregarious birds were, indeed, finding food and sharing it
with flock-mates. Heinrich added an interesting insight into
the courtship patterns of ravens when he wrote:

> "Consider the case of the raven in winter: During this
> season when ravens breed, the male must provide
> carcasses, at least for part if not all of the food supply
> during the incubation period. What would determine
> his acquisition of food? First, the ability to hold a
> territory, which should depend on dominance over
> other birds who might contest either the territory
> directly or food bonanzas within it. Second, the
> ability to find carcasses, which in turn would depend
> upon good eyesight and vigorous flight to cover large
> distances. Third, daring (or experience) to approach
> objects that could be food without getting killed in
> the process. All of these qualities would be essential in
> a mate. . . ." (HEINRICH, 1989)

Raven Romance

While mated pairs of ravens can be seen throughout the year, an imperceptible change occurs in February. An unusual variety of metallic and melodious sounds resonate through the early spring air: it is courtship time. With the season comes the incredible aerobatics of ravens in love. Driven by an inborn survival imperative, unmated birds seek the one who will share nesting responsibilities, the one with whom to raise chicks. Flying more closely together than normally, wing to wing, they somersault, barrel roll, fly high above the chosen one and dive like thunderbolts. They pair off and perch together in trees, allopreening, making sweet sounds, and rubbing one another's bills in a type of "eskimo kiss." (Perhaps these Arctic peoples learned this kiss from Raven, Creator of the World?)

Close scientific observations of raven courtship have been chronicled by Kilham, Heinrich, Lorenz, and a number of other naturalists. But as is true with human love, very little is known as to why or how specific ravens select specific mates. Female ravens are able to test their potential providers, as Heinrich described:

"Finding and winning a proper mate is an important event, which many animals execute with considerable energy and inventive expertise.... Some females can raise a family without a mate's help, but a female raven is utterly dependent on her male for food over a month of every year. As one might expect in birds who rely on their mates to feed them and their young, evolution has provided safeguards in the courting behavior that helps a female assess whether or not a suitor is going to be a good provider. It is done by a very 'clever' ploy. During courtship the female acts like a helpless fledgling, mimicking both the behavior and voice of the begging young. The evolutionary rationale is that if the male can provide for her when she mimics a fledgling, he can probably provide later for her and hers as well.... Almost nothing is known about the basis on which ravens choose mates. We can only make intelligent guesses based on the well-developed theory of mate choice as it applies to other birds. One thing is sure, part of the choice is, at least in the immediate sense, related to displays that bring attention to suitors...." (HEINRICH, 1989)

Raven Humor

Like crows, ravens seem to have a highly developed sense of humor; they play with their siblings, mates, and a wide variety of animals. Ravens have been observed on a cold winter day waiting to slide down a snowy incline, taking turns for a spin down the snow "slide." There are also published accounts of wild ravens stealing fish from otters. Working in pairs, one raven will pull the otter's tail shortly after the otter emerges from the stream with a fresh fish. The otter will drop the fish and turn to face the mischievous intruder, at which point the other raven swoops down and grabs the fish. They are not only teasing the otter, but are also helping themselves to the benefits of his hard work.

Dr. Kilham first studied ravens while on an expedition to northern Iceland. His first direct encounter while hunting a raven indicated to him that ravens will tease other animals not only for food but because they find it amusing.

"In the year after I was graduated from Harvard, I was taken on an expedition to northern Greenland, a part of the arctic that few have had a chance to visit. My job was to collect birds and mammals for the Museum of Comparative Zoology. I do not like to shoot things, but in those days, 1933, there was little talk about ecology and conservation. Our last stop before heading for the pack ice was Isafiord, in northern Iceland. About two hundred ravens, tame as chickens, swarmed on a shingle where fish were cleaned. I could not shoot one there with so many people around, nor could I elsewhere, for once away from town, the ravens became wild and difficult to approach.

"Then one morning I seemed to have a chance. I had climbed up the inland plateau and was walking about when a raven came circling overhead. That was it. I lifted my single-barrel, 20-gauge shotgun and fired. One small feather drifted down as the raven continued circling, seemingly undisturbed. I lowered my gun, searched my pocket for another shell, and was reloading when I looked up. The raven was back sooner than I expected. Just as I looked up he took a shot at me. A large, purplish splotch (the raven had been eating crowberries) landed on the front of my hat. I took it off and gazed in astonishment. One can say that it was all fortuitous, but that is not the way it seemed to me. The experience left me with a feeling that ravens, in addition to being sharp mentally, may have a sense of humour...." (KILHAM, 1989)

Raven Play

Like human children, and the young of other species, young ravens develop their agility, reflexes, and muscle tone through play. Not only is it an expression of higher intelligence, it is also a preparation for life in the wild.

Ravens bond, display affection, and play with their parents and mates. Hand-raised ravens operate in a similar fashion with the individual or family who rears them. Like crows, ravens play with coyotes and wolves as well. Some very beautiful accounts have been given by Koyukon and other arctic and sub-arctic peoples who believe that ravens bring good luck in a hunt, if prayed to properly. Many native hunters offer prayers to Raven before, during, and after a hunt, because they believe that ravens can show them where to find the deer or caribou or elk; divine Raven can place a spell over the prey, holding it long enough for the human hunter to make his kill. Raven then expects a share of the meat for his help. A symbiosis exists between humans and ravens and ravens and wolves, for a similar reason: one "partner" provides the other with a service that multiplies the ability of both to secure food, and thus survive.

Native peoples feel that ravens lead wolves to potential prey such as caribou in the deep winter, also that ravens listen to the howling of wolf packs that indicates they have brought down something, and fly to share in the feast. In a book entitled *In Praise of Wolves*, by R.D. Lawrence, descriptions of wolf and raven hunting, bonding, and concerts beneath the Midnight Sun were presented. Lawrence and his wife lived in the Yukon, where they raised two wolf cubs. They kept these cubs in a wire enclosure, and each afternoon, nine ravens came to keep them company. The wolves and the ravens sang together in the gathering dark, and the ravens vocalized with each other after the communal chorus ended.

"Nothing is more haunting, spiritual, and primitive than the calls of ravens and wolves coming at the same time from the same location," Lawrence wrote.

"A wild concert not infrequently heard during the breeding season of wolves and after a pack has made a kill. . .
the ravens respond. . . each uttering its own particular
repertoire of gurgling notes, bell-like sounds, and slurred
chatter that to my ears is akin to human language. . . ."

In the great white North, ravens and wolves play a kind of tag
in which ravens wait for wolves to fall asleep and then pounce
upon them as they slumber, pulling tails or ears; they are, in
turn, chased by the annoyed wolves. It is a game with no clear
food or survival benefit, but one that is apparently entertain-
ing for both. Ravens will also chase wolves, flying above their
heads, out of the reach of snapping jaws. In his study of
raven-and-wolf interplay, L.D. Mech explained that ravens
and wolves travel together and seem to enjoy interacting with
one another.

"The birds would dive at a wolf's head or tail and the
wolf would duck and then leap at them. . . .When
the wolf retaliated by stalking the raven, the bird
allowed it within a foot before arising. Then it landed a few feet beyond the wolf, and repeated the prank.
. . . It appears that the wolf and the raven have reached
an adjustment in their relationships such that each
creature is rewarded in some way by the presence of
the other and that is fully aware of the other's capabil-
ities. Both species are extremely social, so they must

possess the psychological mechanisms necessary for
forming social attachments. Perhaps in some way
individuals of each species have included members of
the other in their social group and have formed bonds
with them." (MECH, 1970)

Another interesting thing is that, if allowed to roam freely,
wolves and ravens will find each other, even in human neigh-
borhoods. A hand-raised raven, Raveny, who became a member of the Kilham family, attracted young wolves who lived
with a man at a farm near the Kilham's house in Lyme. Dr.
Kilham said that one day he looked out at Raveny's aviary,
and there sitting beside it were two wolves.

As noted earlier in the book by Dr. Kilham, young ravens
taken in by human families bond with people; they assume
that the human family is their own and integrate into the
family structure, becoming defenders of the household and
its members. Intelligent and oriented toward family units,
ravens make excellent companions, both for each other and
for people. A New Mexico raven (later named Clem) was
adopted by a family after it was found blown out of its nest
during a fierce March storm. Clem's mother had built her
nest high in a pine tree, but it was not well sheltered. Clem
was the only simp to survive out of a clutch of four.

Adopted into a human family, Clem had been with his
new family for a month when the couple's first child, a girl,
was born. Clem and the baby grew up together, and Clem
was the consummate babysitter. He watched after the baby in
her cradle, and as she grew and became a toddler, kept her

company and brought her apples from the family orchard.
Whenever a car drove up the family road, or strangers—
human or animal—came toward the little girl, Clem
announced the intruder.

> "Clem is protective of Tamar. While we worked
> outdoors we draped a piece of cheesecloth over her
> basket to keep bugs away. Clem pulled it off and sat
> perched on the side of the basket, on guard duty, his
> big black feet gripping the basket edge, his body
> tipping this way and that as he tried to maintain his
> balance. . . . If Tamar was indoors in her cradle, Clem
> often sat under it. If Tamar cried, he paced in circles
> around and around—especially when her crying went
> on for some time. When she quieted down, Clem
> stopped pacing. . . ." (DEWEY, 1986)

Clem stayed with the family for two years, then returned to
the wild of his own volition one fall.

Young ravens explore their world after fledging, visiting
various food and watering sites, enjoying attractive views,
keeping wary eyes out for danger. Ravens seem to enjoy color
and excitement, and the activity of human crowds is very
appealing to them—when they can watch from a safe distance.
A mated pair of ravens frequents a section of Flagstaff's
Northern Arizona University campus where the chemistry,
biology, and liberal arts departments are housed. Every day,
the bright-eyed pair perches high atop the chemistry building;
they watch the movement of students, visit dumpsters, and

waddle across the grounds between classes. Other ravens perch on top of street lights along busy Flagstaff avenues, observing the movement of cars in between snacks at fast-food restaurant trash cans.

Ravens, Curiosity, and Fear

People who live close to animals in the natural world know that intelligence and fear, like intelligence and curiosity, are closely related; fear is an effective survival tool. Young ravens are interested in their world, but they are very timid around things that they have never seen before. For example, a group of young ravens were terrified of a towel hanging on a clothesline. Why? It was big and white and it flapped in the wind. To the ravens, it must have appeared to be a menace.

Although wild ravens and crows both love snow—they slide in it, jump into snowbanks, and bathe in it—Dr. Kilham's Raveny was terrified by the first snowfall he experienced in Lyme. Raveny slept in a shed behind the farmhouse. According to Dr. Kilham, Raveny refused to emerge from his shed during the first snow. He came to the door, looked out and then ran crying to a favorite hiding place. Once he became used to snow, however, he enjoyed it as other ravens do.

The author once saw a raven sitting in a tree staring at a large, red, metal toy fire-truck. In the sunlight, the truck's chrome shimmered and the red paint glinted and gleamed. After watching it for a while, the raven tried to approach the truck. It flew from the tree and gingerly waddled toward the beautiful object of raven desire. It never got close enough to touch the toy, however. It approached, jumped back, and then retreated to the tree, mumbling to itself. The bird clearly coveted the little truck, but was unsure about its safety. Could this be a new way to trap an unwary raven? Finally, fear overcame desire and the raven flew away, abandoning the tempting prize.

The caution of ravens has not gone unnoticed among American Indians. Koyukon people honor Great Raven as Creator of the World, and call Great Raven's descendants *dotson*. While they greet ravens, pray to them for luck, and respect them, the Koyukon also know them very well. They have observed both the birds' fear and courage.

One of their stories concerns the Distant Time, when Raven was living with his nephew, the mink.

> "Raven liked this arrangement because he could eat the fish that Mink cached around the lakes. But after a while he grew tired of fish and suggested that Mink catch a bear. So they made a plan. Raven split a fish wide open, and Mink hid himself inside it; then they put the fish next to a bear trail. When a bear came along, it swallowed the fish, and Mink crawled out of it and cut the bear's insides with his knife, killing it. The next time, it was Raven's turn to hide in the fish. Although he didn't like the idea at all, he finally consented. But when the bear came along and was about to grab the fish, Raven suddenly jumped out, and with a loud, frightened *Kwaawk!* flew away. That's how ravens are, always afraid."   (R. K. Nelson, 1983)

Ravens use fear of the unknown as an advisor: better to fly away in fear than be drawn in by curiosity or hunger and die. Fearlessness can lead to death. For example, as has been mentioned, ravens love the sound, feel, and taste of water. Young ravens are particularly attracted to it, and sometimes wade or jump into water that is fast-moving or deep, panic, and drown.

Fear has a role in the lives of all birds, not just corvids. Each day holds the unknown and the potential for sudden death. However, fear, essential for avian survival, is forgotten when it comes to defending territory, mates, and chicks. At such times, corvids are staunch and determined.

Food Caching and Gluttony

Like their crow cousins, ravens will deliberately hide food that they cannot quickly consume, saving it for times when food is not so accessible. Ravens hide food in snowbanks, in trees, and between rocks; they will also dig holes in leaf piles and in the ground. Ravens spy on crows and loot crow caches, and join the fracas at wolf and coyote kills, helping themselves to fresh meat, carrying some away and caching it.

Ravens are also notorious gluttons, despite the foresight they display in caching. Juvenile ravens are frequently observed gobbling enormous quantities of food, caching some, and coming back to eat more. In the case of one hand-raised raven, a neighboring dog's food bowl was a reliable second larder. The juvenile raven would fly over to the dog's bowl and consume every bit of food as the dog patiently watched.

At times, the bird was so stuffed that he could not fly home, at which time, he would tap at the neighbor's back door and cry to be carried back across the street to his home. Regardless of the amount of food the raven's adopted family fed him, he continued his gastronomical forays until the neighbors started feeding their dog inside the house. Raven gluttony can be truly spectacular.

Studying
Nature

*W*estern science includes a school of thought that strives to quantify everything and reduce life to statistics, graphs, and line drawings. These scientists, termed "behaviorists," discount the possibility that higher animals can think or feel emotion. They insist that everything animals do is an instinct or survival reaction. They also discount independent and creative animal thinking.

Behavorists view indigenous interpretations of crows and ravens as "folklore," and consider observations of raven ingenuity, humour, and affection "anthropomorphic." They generally separate themselves from nature and its denizens and say that humankind alone has deductive reasoning and higher emotions. Surely they have never observed ravens flying and tumbling in play, or seen the teasing interaction of ravens and wolves. While quantitative biological analysis plays an important role in research, and contributes to overall knowledge, it is the author's opinion that, in order to understand the natural world, one must walk in that world.

Ancient societies and contemporary indigenous cultures do not discount animal intelligence and emotions. Once, when a Hopi *kikmongwi* (father of the village, the highest theocratic office) came to visit and see two crows in the process of rehabilitation, it was mentioned to him that the birds had started talking, meaning that they were imitating human speech. He turned and said, "Why of course, we Hopis have known that for a long time. They tell us lots of things, you just have to listen." Obviously on separate wave-lengths, but the difference between European-influenced thoughts and traditional Native American thought was quite clear in that brief interchange.

A more holistic and reality-based alternative to European philosophy and behavorialism is to touch the earth and the creatures that inhabit it. One must see them and respect them. Animal or avian behavior cannot be understood only through what is observed and recorded in a laboratory. While much is learned from studying, living, and caring for captive and injured animals, the combination of care, captive observation, and field observation seems to be the true key to a better understanding of the world, and the role each element—human, animal, avian, reptile, and plant—plays in the intricate web of life.

Ethology, the study of animal behavior and motivation, may have been recently integrated into western science, but it is indeed an ancient study. From the beginning of human societies, people have lived beside, depended upon, and studied animals. It is only comparatively recently that human beings have separated themselves from the rest of the natural world.

Some have ascribed the ability to communicate with other animals as magic. It is said that King Solomon had a magic ring, given to him by his lover the Queen of Sheba that allowed him to speak and understand all of the languages of animals. Nobel Prize–winning naturalist Konrad Lorenz explained this talent in a different way.

"As Holy Scripture tells us, the wise King Solomon, the son of David, spake also of beasts, and of fowl, and of creeping things, and of fishes.... A slight misreading of this text, which very probably is the oldest record of a biological lecture, has given rise to the charming legend that the king was able to talk the language of animals, which was hidden from all other men.... I am quite ready to believe that Solomon really could do so, even without the help of the magic ring which is attributed to him by the legend in question, and I have very good reason for crediting it; I can do it myself, and without the aid of magic, black or otherwise. I do not think it is very sporting to use magic rings in dealing with animals. Without supernatural assistance, our fellow creatures can tell us the most beautiful stories, and that means true stories, because the truth about nature is always far more beautiful even than what our great poets sing of it, and they are the only real magicians that exist...."
(LORENZ, 1952)

Corvids
and the Law

Law is probably one of the most profoundly human creations of all. Through laws humans attempt to regulate innumerable activities, behaviors, and responses. These attempts are not confined to human activities, but extend to the natural world and human interaction with it. In some cases, laws function as critically needed protective barriers between people and the rest of the planet's inhabitants. In other instances, they function as incomprehensible obstructions.

In 1972, the United States Congress approved the Migratory Bird Treaty Act. Under its terms and the treaty the United States entered into with Great Britain, her Canadian dominions, Mexico, and Japan, federal protection was provided to all wild birds in the United States and its territories; resident game birds such as pheasant, grouse, and quail (managed by respective states) and the English sparrow, starling, and the feral pigeon are excepted from this protection.

While migratory bird hunting regulations do allow the taking of some game birds at specified times and locations, the bottom line under treaty provisions is that it is unlawful for anyone to kill, capture, collect, possess, buy, sell, trade, ship, import, or export any bird covered by the provisions of the act, unless an appropriate federal permit (and in most cases, a state permit) is obtained first.

Doubtless the intent of the law and the treaty was good, but often the practical result is that anyone who stops to help a wounded bird without first obtaining a federal and/or state permit is violating the law. A compassionate person, by taking in and assisting in the healing and rehabilitation of an injured protected bird is in fact a criminal, unless, of course, that person has applied for and been granted federal and state permits. Most Americans are not aware of the laws, and federal and state game officials point out that if a person finds a hurt bird and brings it to the officers, the Good Samaritan will not be prosecuted.

If the bird is not on the endangered species list and a local rehabilitation center has room for it, it will be taken in and treated. Caring for hurt birds is a time-consuming and risky proposition. Often, by the time it reaches competent care-takers, the bird has been so weakened or so badly injured that it dies. With rehabilitation training and the appropriate per-mits, both caretakers and patients have a better chance for success and security.

Rehabilitators are trained and approved by federal officials and given permits, which must be renewed annually, to care for birds. An individual licensed rehabilitator is allowed to work with an injured bird for 90 days, and must request an extension if the bird has not healed and able to return to the wild in that time. In the case of endangered bird species, the

rehabilitator is allowed an automatic 180 days to work with
the bird. If it is finally judged to be non-releasable, it can be
used in captive breeding and foster-parent programs for
endangered bird chicks.

Under normal circumstances, a bird so badly damaged
that it will never be able to be returned to the wild is considered non-releasable. Such birds must be placed in zoos or in
public educational programs if they are to survive. Otherwise,
"something must be done," which is often a euphemism for
official killing of the bird. Federal regulations do not provide
rest or retirement homes for crippled, non-releasable birds.

It is clearly stipulated in the regulations that "a special-
purpose permit may be issued to an applicant who submits a
written application containing the general information. . .
and makes a sufficient showing of benefit to the migratory
bird resource, important research reasons, reasons of human
concern for individual birds, or other compelling justification."*

Until about the mid-1980s, permits for humanitarian
concerns were freely given to applicants who filled out the
papers and paid the $25 license fee. The decision to approve
or disapprove humanitarian permits for individual birds has
traditionally been left up to the federal area directors, and
these directors set the humanitarian permit policy for their

---

*This is taken directly from the federal regulations about migratory birds.
According to an Albuquerque-based United States Fish and Wildlife Officer,
it was once common for humane permits to be given out, but it is now
almost impossible to get one.

regions. Of the seven district offices in the United States, five (including the one in Albuquerque, New Mexico) have a standard procedure of denying permits, even though the regulations stipulate that they may be issued. There are, of course, appeal processes, and ultimately, some decisions may be made directly by the Secretary of the Interior.

There are several levels of federal and state bureaucracy that the private citizen must broach for humanitarian permits, rehabilitator's licenses, research and collection permits, falconry permits, import and export permits, banding and marking permits, taxidermy permits, waterfowl sale and disposal permits, and a mysterious "special purpose" permit, described as given for "certain special actions involving migratory birds for which a standard form permit has not been provided, such as: salvage of sick, injured, or dead birds; experimental breeding of migratory game birds other than waterfowl; unusual possession, transportation or display needs, etc., for which, in amply justified situations, a special permit may be provided. . . "

There are even permits to shoot depredating crows or other protected birds, if non-lethal means have not been successful in keeping them away from agriculture. The average American would have a difficult time navigating this confusing and overwhelming labyrinth.

Both federal officials and the regulations stress that all states have similar provisions for most migratory birds and that a federal permit is not valid without a corresponding state permit. Here arises the catch-22: state officials say they cannot issue a permit unless federal officers have granted the permit-seeker their approval, and federal officers frequently say they cannot give permission until the state officials have issued a permit. A circular paper chase can ensue unless one has a skilled attorney or has been through the process before.

Where does this leave the person who finds an injured corvid? Be aware that if a bird is rescued, the rescuer is technically in violation of the law unless, of course, a permit is in hand. The bird assisted may ultimately be confiscated and killed.

Wildlife belongs free and in Nature, and proper care and rehabilitation can help this happen. But what about crippled, "non-releasables"? Perhaps the solution lies in equal administration of regulations. Certainly anyone who would invest the time, attention, and expense necessary and then endure the elaborate rituals of federal and state paperwork would be unlikely to be irresponsible or neglectful. Further, the regulations stipulate yearly inspections and visits by local game officials; if the caretaker were found to be neglectful or exploitive, it would be reasonable for the state to remove the animal from the individual's custody. At the very least, the status of humanitarian permits should be re-examined. Many rehabilitators would be happy to care forever for non-releasables. This is in both letter and spirit of the law.

MODERN MANIFESTATIONS

Today's World

From the dawn of human religious experience, people have made prayers to the Raven and the Crow. Depictions of these sacred birds appear in carved inscriptions, in Palaeolithic cave frescoes, in Australian aboriginal paintings from the Dreamtime. The sanctity of Raven and Crow is honored throughout the world. From the earliest African and Asiatic hunters to the Celtic bards and healers and the indigenous mystics of North America, humans have recognized the unique powers of these corvids. Among the first people to recognize their special status were the shamans.

A shaman, who is a person with the ability to commune with the Spirit World, the world of deities and natural forces, intercedes with entities seen and unseen in order to heal the sick, ensure good hunting, and protect fellow human beings from malevolent forces, while placating the powers and asking for help from benevolent ones. Shamans develop personal relationships with the Spirit World, and through these relationships, they promote harmony in this world, ensuring the survival of their fellow humans.

In some societies, shamans come from long lines of religious leaders; in others, a person is chosen for this role by the gods and spirits themselves. The common thread in shamanic experience is that the shaman receives knowledge and learns directly from the entity or entities who are his or her spiritual allies. This knowledge frequently comes through dreams and visions, usually after a personal crisis due to fasting, utilization of hallucinogens, or an illness in which the individual crosses over into the Spirit World and is brought back to this world through the intercession of the mystic ally. While the spirits are considered to be all around and no real dividing point between this world and the Spirit World is perceived, the shaman is in closer touch with these forces than is the common person.

A spiritual ally is a supernatural being, a being that can come in many forms (often an animal or bird), whose intercession and assistance with the Divine World are absolutely essential for shamanic success. Sometimes this ally is the essence of the animal in whose form it manifests itself, sometimes it appears in its own spiritual form. The jaguar, for example, is a powerful shamanic ally among the tribes of Central and South America. In Beringia and China, the goose and gander are popular.

Several different types of birds assist the shaman; bird feathers have special powers, powers that can lift the shaman up and away from the earthbound world into vastly different realms and then return the healer safely back home. Alone of all the Bird People, crows and ravens can cross between the

world of the living and the world of the dead. For this and
many other reasons they are among the most important of
shamanic birds. Shamans develop deep personal relationships
with their spiritual allies, and they gain knowledge through
actively seeking contact with the divine world—they gain
knowledge through acquisition and suffering and the grace of
the spirits. If a shaman is fortunate enough to have Crow or
Raven as an ally, the person has great power.

Religious scholars say that shamanism is largely associated
with hunting and gathering societies; such cultures are highly
individualistic and need people of power—shamanic medicine people—who can directly intervene between the human
and the spirit worlds through their magic. They say that when
human beings developed agricultural societies and sedentary
village lifeways, new types of religious needs evolved, and new
types of religious societies emerged. These were the first
priesthoods.

A priest/priestess acquires knowledge through training
and learning—from human beings and the Mystic. Priests are
trained and initiated by other priests into religious societies
and extensive religious specialization evolves. For example,
some priesthoods concentrate on healing the sick, some on
ensuring the germination of crops, some on caring for the
dead and their funerary rights, and so on. As the agricultural
cycle of planting, crop care, and harvest dictates human life
and timetables, it also affects human religious views.

Many groups gradually adapted agricultural cultures,
settling in villages, living according to the cycles of the seasons

and how these seasons affected their corn, beans, and squash in the New World, wheat and barley in the Old World. As people began to separate from the natural environment, they became manipulators of Nature rather than integrated components of it. In the structured village theocracies arising in the New and Old worlds, there was little room for strong individualism and wild shamanic rituals. Priests needed to be able to predict and control the rain, the germination of crops. They looked to the stars, the moon, and the sun for instruction. Great cyclical ceremonial calenders evolved, with crops and agricultural cycles at their very hearts.

Religious formulas were developed in which magic was institutionalized and rituals memorized by all initiates in order to provide for the future of their peoples. Priestly societies gathered and developed not only religious and ritual knowledge, but also natural scientific, astronomical, and astrological knowledge—the cycles of flood and rain, drought, and famine. Initiates into priestly societies gained access to the accumulated knowledge of the past and utilized it for magical and village survival purposes.

The first great civilizations emerged from these agricultural societies. Because people learned farming did not mean shamanic ritual ended. In many priesthoods, shamanic elements were incorporated, and in societies like China, Taoism, essentially a shamanic philosophy, survived changing cultural patterns by incorporating elements of both hunter and farmer religions.

Examples of the blending of shaman and priest can be found in Navajo medicine men, who are taught strict rituals, ritual behavior, and the formulas of ritual, but at the same time act as intermediaries between the human and the Mystic. They emerged in the Great Southwest as a people whose basic rituals were first shamanic, and gradually, through the instructions of their Holy People and the sharing of religious and agricultural knowledge with their Pueblo neighbors (who were theocratic farmers), evolved into the complex and elaborate songs and healing chants of today.

Even though today's is a post-agricultural and a post-industrial world, priests and shamans are still active in it. Through direct personal intercession with the Mystic and the help of spiritual allies, the modern shaman makes people well and restores harmony to the world. The priest is still initiated by other priests and taught the proper religious formulas to restore universal balance and harmony, and his voice still sings among the world's peoples.

Raven shamans and priests are found today from Siberia across into Beringia and into North America. Kwakiutl dancers become ravens. Yaqui shamans take peyote or datura and transform into crows to do their spiritual work. Raven priests offer tobacco to the gods in Mexico and Central America. Priests and priestesses dance for House Crows during autumn festivals in Bali, and they serve Kali and Shiva in India. Raven religion survives in its many manifestations.

Make Prayers
to the Raven

The Raven religion is strong throughout North America, particularly among the tribes of the Pacific Northwest Coast and Alaska. People from many Indian cultures make prayers to the Raven, and both Raven and Crow are revered as medicine birds. One shaman who works with the power of Raven and Crow is Medicine Grizzly Bear (whose everyday name is Bobby Lake), employed in Indian Education at a university in Spokane, Washington. When telephoned for an appointment for an interview, he said, "Listen, can you hear that?" and held the phone away from himself. A cacophony of corvid calls came through the telephone line.

"Do you hear that raven and that crow? They are in the tree outside of the window here. Of course I will talk to you, they're jumping up and down and hollering and telling me to talk to you."

Medicine Grizzly Bear is of Seneca and Cherokee descent, a medicine man by training and acquisition, married to a California Yurok medicine woman from a long line of healers. Medicine Grizzly Bear makes prayers to the Raven, and offers unique insights into how Raven walks among his people today.

"To me, the Raven is sacred, *Quigok* is his name. We call him *Quigok-kegae,* which means the doctor bird. My elders have taught me and I've come to learn that Raven is the Great Creator's partner," Medicine Grizzly Bear explained. "Raven not only helped create this world, but has more power than any of the other birds on the face of the earth.

"Everybody thinks the Eagle has so much power—that the Eagle can see the farthest, can fly the highest, is the most courageous, the strongest, the biggest, and most beautiful bird. And all native people, no matter where you go in North and South America, want eagle feathers. They think the Eagle is the most important. Well, in some respects, that may be true, but he is not the *most* powerful. The raven is the only bird that has enough power to go over into the land of the deceased and bring a person's soul back."

The priest explained that not all medicine people have the power to revive a person, to bring their soul back from the Spirit World once they have crossed into the land of the dead, but if a healer has access to the power of Raven, it *is* possible, and he himself has utilized that power.

"If you are connected to Raven and Raven works with you as a spiritual ally and you have his or her song and power and knowledge, when a person is dying, you can activate the power of Raven to go over into the land of the deceased and bring them back to life—that's how much power that bird has," Medicine Grizzly Bear stated with conviction. "To the best of my knowledge, none of the other birds can do this, not even Eagle."

The Raven priest said that he had called on Raven to
bring people's souls back from the spirit world three times,
twice in situations with his wife, who had been pronounced
clinically dead, and once with his father, who had suffered a
brain hemorrhage and was dying in an intensive care unit
in Santa Monica, California.

"The only thing that was keeping him alive was a life
support system. The doctors—white doctors—wouldn't let
me do a ceremony [at his father's bedside] because of the
oxygen and all the stuff that was in there. So I went outside
and I prayed, right in the heart of the city. I went out and I
prayed and I talked to the Creator and asked Raven to help
me. By the time I got back upstairs, on the fourth or fifth
floor of the intensive care unit, there were four ravens sitting
on the windowsill there, right by my father's bed, and he
came out of the coma. That's power.

"I'll tell you something else about Raven that people don't
understand, why he's the most powerful bird. You can go as
far north as you possibly can, go to the coldest place on the
face of the earth, wherever it may be. . . go as far as you can
go, where there is nothing else living, not even a polar bear. . .
and you look around and right there is that raven. Now you
can go just the opposite. You can go all the way down into
the Mojave Desert, or the worst desert in the world, where it is
so hot, so hot that you won't even find a lizard panting, and
there is that raven. You can go to the worst jungle, into a
jungle where there are the deadliest insects and snakes and creatures and monsters, the most dangerous creatures, and there

is that raven. Or you could go into the largest city in the United States—New York, Los Angeles, Chicago, Baltimore, any dirty, polluted [place], you know, just a cesspool of society, and there's that raven. The other birds can't do that. They don't have that kind of power. But Raven can do it, he is a survivor. He helped create this world with the Great Creator. So."

Medicine Grizzly Bear explained that in addition to making prayers to Raven, people should honor the crow as well. "Crow is the Raven's little brother or sister. The crow is a different kind of power. The crow is warrior power, used for warrior medicine and for protection. During World War II and Vietnam, some of my friends and uncles and relations and people had to go to war—they didn't want to, but they had to go. So the medicine people would get together and they'd sing and they'd pray over them and they'd use the crow feathers and the crow medicine and place that protection over the people going off to war. They sang the wardance song and used crow medicine on that person so when they went to war, they wouldn't get killed, they'd came back home."

Medicine Grizzly Bear said that once the G.I.s returned from the wars, medicine people conducted purification ceremonies, again calling on the power of Crow. The men cleansed themselves in the sweat lodge and prayed and sang, purging the returning warriors of the horrible experiences of war and killing. "It was the power of Crow that saved them," the priest reaffirmed.

The ubiquitous presence of the crow serves as a key to the bird's success. "You see, nobody notices the crow, but the crow is all over. He is inconspicuous, you know, and some people think he's a pest, he's so common. People don't notice them, but the crows see everything and remember things and gossip among themselves about events all over the world. Sorcerers, too, [the people we call] sorcerers—the Indian devil, the people who work with the black magic part, the black arts part of native medicine and knowledge—they work with the power of Crow. You know, they can turn into a crow, or they can merge their consciousness with the crow and sneak up on people or play tricks on people or hurt people if they want to, because nobody notices the crow," Medicine Grizzly Bear said.

He explained that the crow itself is not evil, that only wicked people with their own nefarious plans are evil. "But by the same token, a good medicine person, a high spiritual healer, can merge their consciousness with Raven (or could in the olden days, I don't know if anybody can do this now), they could actually go through a complete physical metamorphosis and turn into a raven and fly somewhere to doctor a person, or to see what they want to see, or to gain knowledge or check up on things and come back."

Medicine Grizzly Bear said that although he has not been given the gift of transformation, he does merge his consciousness with ravens during healing ceremonies, and through such merging, the ravens help him reach patients far from his home in Spokane. "Fact, fiction, fantasy, magic, who knows? There are forms of knowledge that some of our native people have that go beyond Western realities; Western science hasn't developed the knowledge or skill to catch up with it. So."

Medicine Grizzly Bear explained that Raven and Crow can not only help the living, but their power can help relieve the suffering of the unquiet dead as well. He told of a healing episode, in which his wife, through her spiritual alliance with Raven, helped the ghost of a little girl cross over from this earthly plane into the Spirit World. The little Anglo-American child had been killed on a road not far from Medicine Grizzly Bear's home. The medicine people had heard about the tragedy, but didn't know the family involved. Shortly after the accident, a little girl visited them every night in their bedroom, awakening them with her crying. They finally realized that this was a ghost-child, and they calmed her down and spoke with her, and asked her what was wrong and what they could do to help her.

The ghost-girl told the couple that she had been hit by a car, and she was lost and frightened, she didn't know what to do or where to go. Eventually, the lost soul's parents sought the advice and guidance of the Yurok healer. They asked Medicine Grizzly Bear's wife to conduct a ceremony and help the ghost-girl cross over into the Spirit World.

The bereaved and suffering family offered the medicine woman a gift of tobacco, and the Yurok healer agreed to undertake the difficult job. Medicine Grizzly Bear said that his wife started her prayers that night as she built a fire. "She asked the Creator and the ancestors and the spirits to go and get that little girl and escort her over to the land of the deceased, where she belonged," the shaman explained.

"Dead people don't belong on the Earth plane. It was at

night, and this is the first time I ever saw anything like this happen. When she built her fire and started her prayers, four ravens came in—this was about eleven or twelve o'clock at night—and just hollered. The four ravens circled around the family and if you had. . . the [mystical] ability to see, you could see that little girl travelling with those ravens, heading up toward the sky at nighttime, and then, as they got up toward the Milky Way, a shooting star shot real fast, and that was the last of the problem. I'd never seen ravens come out at nighttime like that," Medicine Grizzly Bear concluded.

The priest said that while this ghost experience was the first time he had seen ravens come out at night, there was one other time when a raven came out at night—on the eve of his second daughter's birth. "The only other time in my life I saw a raven at night was when I was seeking a vision to name my second daughter," Medicine Grizzly Bear said. "My wife was in the hospital giving birth to our daughter and I was in the sweat lodge, fasting and praying for her. So while she was in pain and sweating and fasting in her labor, I was in the sweat house and I was fasting and sweating. While she was praying and seeking a vision with the Grandmother spirits to help her have an easy childbirth, I was in the sweat lodge, praying for her and the newborn. But I also sought a vision. Inside the sweat lodge, it was dark except for the glowing hot rocks and the steam. It was just like turning on a television set in my mind. I heard this raven calling, and I looked around the sweat lodge and opened my eyes—I didn't see anything, and I really thought it [the raven] was outside. And then, what I saw was a full moon, and I saw this big, female raven standing in the middle of this full moon.

"And I told her 'Well, Grandmother, what are you trying to tell me?' and she said, 'This is what we want you to name your daughter: *Ya-naas-lah-quigok.* In the Yurok language, that means Moon Raven, and we will give your daughter those powers. She will have the power to work with the moon and she will have the power to work with the ravens,' the Grandmother told me," Medicine Grizzly Bear continued.

"And she does. She's only nine years old and she has that."

Medicine Grizzly Bear said that after the vision conversation, he left the sweat lodge and was getting ready to jump into the creek when he heard a raven "hollering."

"It was the same raven that I saw in my mind. There were other [people] with me, and we turned around when we heard this raven, and we looked at the sweat lodge. And on top of my sweat lodge was a big raven and a full moon right behind her. So if I had any doubts, the reality in the physical sense was right there," Medicine Grizzly Bear concluded.

The Raven priest said that the next morning he went to see his wife in the hospital to discuss the vision with her and make arrangements for the naming of the child. "She already knew what the name was going to be, because there was a big raven jumping up and down with her, right there by the window in her hospital," Medicine Grizzly Bear said.

"She said, 'I knew you were going to call her Raven something or another.' "

Medicine Grizzly Bear continued his discourse on Raven,

explaining that the raven is an intelligent, magical bird, with powers that people cannot even begin to comprehend. He said that some tribes view Raven as a trickster, because he enjoys teasing and taking advantage of others. "But by his antics and his tricks and his behavior, he becomes a role model for us, he is a teacher to us. People ask how to tell the difference between a raven and a crow. It is hard sometimes to tell the difference between a young raven and an adult crow, but I always tell them, 'Well, look at their aura, and you will see the difference.' The raven has a blue aura and the crow has a black aura. And the raven is of course, bigger, and has a goatee, a much bigger beak, and longer tailfeathers, [which] the crow doesn't. But they are both really powerful birds.

"And if we find one dead, it is an honorable gift and a ceremony [is done] with it. I have a real special respect, a tremendously high regard for Raven and Crow as sacred," Medicine Grizzly Bear concluded. The priest explained that he had a special relationship with Raven since childhood, when Raven saved his life, a total of three times.

The first time occurred when he was a little boy, in the Allegheny Mountains of the Six Nations of the Iroquois Confederation, between New York and Pennsylvania. He was four years old, and had developed a high fever; he recalled seeing little Indians, little people calling him and gesturing for him to follow them. They led the sick child away from his house and deep into the mountain forests. A tremendous lightning and hailstorm raged, and the boy became lost. During the ensuing search, rangers found the boy by following the cries of a raven; the raven was standing protectively on his chest.

Raven helped Medicine Grizzly Bear a second time in his childhood, when the boy tried to save his cousin from drowning, and a third time when he was an adult.

Grizzly Bear said many Indian people make prayers to Raven and ask for his guidance in all situations. "The raven is a counselor and an advisor in a positive sense. He's a sign and an omen, but he advises us. Like when I go hunting. We are taught in the Indian way, you go out and you pray and you make medicine, you talk to the deer and you ask the deer to share its life with you. You just don't go out there and kill it and take the best parts and waste the rest. You pray and you offer it tobacco or different herbs. . . . You make medicine and you ask the deer to share its life, but you also pray to the Raven, to help you to have good luck so you will get the deer. Every time I've done that, when I go out and I pray, I always promise the raven that I will save him the fat around the heart, and some of the other choice pieces of meat. And every time, that raven will show me right where that deer is. He'll be flying right over the top.

"One time I was in a hard, rocky terrain with a lot of brush and trees, and I knew that they [the deer] were there, but I just couldn't get a bead on one. This raven came in, and he just flew around and [called]. That deer was standing there, looking up at that raven. Raven held him captive until I could fire the shot," the shaman said.

Medicine Grizzly Bear stressed that while there are many

different Indian cultures, and many different interpretations of Raven, certain continuities exist in honoring crows and ravens as medicine birds, as representative of that great Raven or Crow who is the divine, mythic deity.

"I'll tell you one last thing," said the Raven priest. "Other Indian people may have different perspectives, because there are different tribal viewpoints.... The way I have been taught and trained by my elders and from my own experience is that the raven represents the last power of Creation, which is the West, water. When we pray, we talk about the four powers of Creation. In the beginning, when the Great Creator first created this world, he called together all of the different spirits. There were as many different spirits as there are stars in the sky. And he asked them what they wanted to be.

"The Four Powers of Creation, as they were in the beginning and they still are today, are: Air, which comes from the North, and the color is white. It represents purity, wisdom, strength and old age. Fire, which comes from the East, and the color is red. It represents rebirth—that's the Great Creator's spirit, the light, the warmth, the Dawn of Enlightenment. It's protection. Earth, which comes from the south and is symbolically represented by the Rock People—all rocks and all solar systems into infinity, and all those things in and around and near the earth. The color is usually yellow, although some might use green for it. That's the warm summer wind, that's the healing wind connected to the earth.

"The last power of Creation is Water, and it comes from the West. It's black, it's darkness, it's the unknown, the Spirit

World, oftentimes symbolically represented by Raven. In
totems and medicine wheels, you will see people using the
bald-headed eagles or the pure white swan for the North; the
flicker-bird or the woodpecker or some other red bird for the
East; for the South, it could be a hummingbird or the yellow
hammer, or some of the other Bird People; and for the West,
it is always the raven. So the black, the mysterious, the unknown, the mystique that surrounds it, connected to lightning and thunder, those are the purifiers.

"When you go to Native rituals and you see these feathers,
they are not just wearing them for looks. They are activating
powers. Just like the psychologist Carl Jung said, these are
universal archetypes, they are the symbols of transformation.
They have meaning, they have purpose, they have function,
and they are doing something. Although other people may
not understand what they are doing, they *are* doing something. And we see a lot of this represented in our Indian heritage and culture," the medicine man emphasized.

"I'm a spiritual person. I do what the spirits tell me. I see
spirits, I hear spirits, they work with me, they work through
me. I honor all of them, but the raven and crow are special to
me. And I call to Raven, I sing the Raven song. I make prayers
to Raven, and Raven answers."

Hopis
and Crows

*W*hile the crow and the raven are respected by most North American tribes, they do not play the same roles in all Indian societies. Among the Hopis of Arizona, crows are viewed with a mixture of respect, amusement, and fear. They sometimes compete with people for corn, and many Hopis farmers view them as pests. Hopis tell stories about the birds, and crows are also closely associated with kachinas.

The Hopi are internally divided into a number of different clan groups, descendants of people who migrated to the Hopi *tutsqua* from many different places. The Crow Clan, *Ungwish-wungwa,* came to the Hopi mesas after the arrival of two other clans, the Strap Clan and the Parrot Clan, according to Hopi priests of the One-Horn Society, a religious fraternity that serves *Masau'u,* God of Life and Death and Lord of This World. Priests of the One-Horn Society learn the origin and migration stories of all the clans. They recite these stories to teach the people their history. Alone of all the Hopi religious priesthoods, the One-Horns can recite these origin stories. Other Hopis are only to know or recite the stories of their own clan.

The Crow Clan came to the mesas from the land around
Arizona's highest mountains, the land upon which modern-
day Flagstaff, Arizona, is built. Rising high above the Colorado
Plateau, above the arid desert floor, is a complex of volcanic
hills today called the San Francisco Peaks. A region of deep
forests, moisture-loving ferns, and refreshing springs, the land
and its vegetation vary from meadow-steppe and yellow
pine to alpine to tundra and snow-capped summits crowned
with jagged rocks. The highest of the mountains, Humphrey
Peak, towers at 12,635 feet.

Hopis know this place as more than a geological anomaly,
the result of volcanic activity. It is *Nuva-tukwa-ovi,* home of
the kachinas. Nuva-tukwa-ovi is populated by thousands of
spirits and divine entities, all sacred and all eternal. Their presence is manifested in the variety of curative and ceremonial
plants, in the bubbling springs, and the voices carried on the
wind. It is a living, holy region. Every year, village priests
make pilgrimages to the water shrines and sacred places up
and down the mountain complex. A feeling of sanctity and
holiness permeates the very air.

To Hopis, all life is one life, the same. No place in this
world, the Fourth World of the Hopi, better illustrates this
than the slopes of Nuva-tukwa-ovi. Hopis say that all things—
people, animals, birds, bugs, plants, trees, even rocks and
stones—share a divine spark, an animated spirit. This divine
spark is called Kachina. Every spring and summer, kachinas
travel from their home in Nuva-tukwa-ovi to visit the dusty
plazas of their Hopi friends and bring Hopi farmers the rain

essential to survival. Hopis believe that all of the outer forms of the animals, the plants, and the rocks are a kind of disguise these entities use when human beings see them. Hopis also say that, in their true forms, these entities appear very much like human beings. The spirits live in a number of parallel worlds, and sometimes, even in the Fourth World, they dissolve their disguises and can be seen in their true forms.

Because all life shares the divine spark, whenever a Hopi collects a plant for healing or ceremonial reasons, cornmeal and often prayer feathers (*pahos*) are offered to the plant's spirit. Cornmeal and pahos are offered to food animals as well, with a sincere prayer of apology and forgiveness from the lips of the hunter. The hunter explains to the animal or plant that he asks the sacrifice of life only for his own survival. A One-Horn priest from Second Mesa once told a story about the San Francisco Peaks and the people who lived there.*

"Listen now—this is the way it was. A long time ago, before the gathering of the clans on the central three mesas of the Hopi *tutsqua*, a small group of dark people lived at the base of *Nuva-tukwa-ovi*. These people were the Crow Clan. Crows and kachinas have always had a special relationship. Sometimes, when crows fly in a flock across the sun, it is like a dark raincloud. Crows love water, and they dearly love corn and

---

*For a more detailed understanding of Hopi religion and Hopi priestly societies, see Edmund Nequatewa, *Truth of a Hopi* (1967, Northland Press).

beansprouts—the same things that people love to eat.

The Mother of All Kachinas is *Angwusi Navasi,*
Crow Mother; she and the crow kachinas are the only
kachinas that wear crow feathers when they manifest
themselves in their divine form to human beings. Members of the Crow Clan were instructed by the kachinas
high on Nuva-tukwa-ovi in how to bring rain through
prayer-dance and ceremonial magic. This was a gift
the kachinas gave to the Crow Clan, because the dark
people showed respect and honor for these spirits long,
long ago. Another gift the kachinas gave the Crow
Clan was their name. After instructing a boy of the
Crow Clan in the way to pray and bring rain, the
kachinas told him that from that time forward, the
Crow Clan and the Kachina would bear the same
name. So it has been."

Crow Mother still comes with her sons into Hopi kivas at
Bean Dance to officiate over initiations. Crow Mother is one
entity, while crow kachinas are another group. Many things
in the Hopi world bear a duality of natures. The living crows
human beings see every day may or may not be kachinas.

To a farming people such as the Hopi, earthly crows can
also be a nuisance. While Hopis do not believe that crows are
bad, they do make pests of themselves, especially around cornfields. Hopis say that in recent years, the numbers of crows
have increased, as have their depredations of Hopi corn fields.
(Coincidentally, in the past year, more and more carvings of

Crow Kachinas have surfaced in the public markets and trading companies of Arizona and New Mexico, perhaps a reflection of Hopi awareness of the crow infestation.)

"A long time ago when I was a little boy growing up, we had crows around here," Oraibi *kikmongwi* Stanley Bahnimptewa explained one winter afternoon. "But back then, the crows showed some respect. They may have hung around the cornfields, but if you asked them to leave, they would go. Today there are so many of them, and they show no respect."

Bahnimptewa and other Hopis said that there could be a number of reasons for the recent infestation of crows. Hopis believe in a world of cause and effect. If people do not do the right things, believe in the right way, natural forces will punish them and remind them of the proper ways. Bahnimptewa said that it is possible that the crows are messengers, sent to remind Hopis to stop fighting with each other, to remind people of the serious drought that has been upon the land for over four years, and to make people remember their obligations. Bahnimptewa, his spokesman Caleb Johnson, and other Hopis have also expressed concern that there may be a darker side to the infestation: a possibility that someone wishes harm to Hopi farmers and Hopi life.

Whatever the reason, Hopis are forced to deal with the rapacious appetites of hungry and aggressive crows. "Why, I saw crows in my cornfields peeling back an ear of corn like it was a banana," one farmer recalled. "I shouted at them. I shooed them. But after my back was turned, they came back."

Another Hopi explained a method he devised to frighten the birds away from his fields.

"What I did was I tied up those aluminum pie pans all along the fence. And then I put out two boom boxes, and I played really loud rock music on them, and I set them in the field. I went and did some things, and when I came back, you should have seen it. The crows were actually attracted by the pretty metal pie pans, and there they were in my cornfield, hopping to the music. It was like a crow disco. It didn't scare them at all. In fact, more crows just kept coming."

Some Hopi farmers said that they had become so desperate to drive away crows that they actually got out their shotguns and shot a few. "We tied their carcasses to the fenceline. The other crows saw them, and stayed away for a few days.

But eventually, they came back and gobbled up the corn. Even the carcasses didn't stop them, because after a while, they were just dry and dusty," a farmer recalled.

The consensus among Hopis was that scarecrows with human forms, clothing, and hats were effective only up to a point. They *have* fooled humans though.

"I know a man with a cornfield not far from my house," Vernon Masayesva said. "One day I saw him working in his field. I saw him standing there and I waved to him. Well, after four or five days, I noticed that he was always standing in the same place: it was a scarecrow wearing his clothes. The scarecrow may not have fooled the crows, but it sure fooled me for a little while," Masayesva laughed.

The general Hopi conclusion about how to deal with crows is best expressed by one Hotevilla farmer. "Yes, yes, the crows come to my corn. I talk to them. I invite them in. I say to them, 'Yes, yes. Come here. Eat, enjoy yourselves. Eat as much as you want. But please, just leave a little bit for me and my family.' "

As can be imagined, crow problems and how to deal with them are widely discussed among people from all three mesas and Moencopi village. Most Hopis admit respect for the crows because of their intelligence and humor, but have some ambivalence about them because, in addition to eating corn and beans, sharing the same foods that human beings eat, they also "eat dead things," and this is something Hopis find repugnant.

Crows and Hopis have a unique relationship that extends beyond the pragmatic to the magical. Stories circulate on the mesas about people who exploit the forms of crows and other animals in order to conduct nefarious nighttime activities. In a classic tale, versions of which exist in every village, a young man falls in love with a beautiful young woman. They marry, and he moves into her house.

At first, married life is blissful. But as time goes by, he notices that his wife is increasingly tired and listless during the day. He knows that she leaves him for long periods at night, always returning just before dawn. He suspects an affair with another man. He decides to follow his wife and find out what is happening.

So one night, on the night of a full moon, he feigns sleep and remains still when his wife brushes a feather over his foot to determine whether he is asleep or awake. When he exhibits no reaction, she assumes that he is asleep. Quietly, she dresses and slips out of their stone house. Quietly, her husband follows her. He follows her through the sleeping village, not to another house, but out beyond the village boundaries. She hastens some distance to an old ruined village—a place uninhabited by people for centuries, now the domain of snakes and ghosts. In these ruins, she is greeted by an older man and a circle of men and women.

The husband becomes far more alarmed at the meeting of a group in darkness and in a dead city than he would be at the discovery of another lover. He begins to fear the worst: that she is in the company of *powacha,* two-hearts—human and animal—humans who transform into animals and prowl the night.

The husband's fears are confirmed when, after chanting

and dancing, the lead male witch brings out a circle hoop.
People begin to jump through the hoop and transform, some
into crows, some into wildcats, some into coyotes and foxes,
some into owls. But their transformations are incomplete. The
crow may have wings, but retains human feet, the wildcat
may have a cat body but a human head, and so on. The lead
witch announces that something is wrong. He tells the others
to jump back through the hoop to regain their human forms.

"Someone is watching. Someone uninitiated into our
secret society. We must find him," the head witch cries. The
group searches through the rocks and ruins, looking for the
one who is spying. The young husband is discovered. He is
forced to make a choice: jump through the hoop, transform,
and become one of them, or die. He jumps through the hoop
and becomes a crow. His wife and the others transform as well.

In her transformed state, the wife plots her husband's
death with the lead witch. The youth overcomes the plot, eventually regains his human form, and overcomes the evil group.

This story and others like it demonstrate Hopi ambivalence toward crows. They stress that crows, as natural creatures, are not evil, but the wicked hearts of men can mani-
pulate living crows and, in cases of witches, the very form of
the crow can be assumed. The crow, by its ubiquitous presence
throughout the mesa country, and indeed, the world, can
travel about with impunity. Humans are so used to crows that
they rarely even notice them. The unscrupulous Two-Heart
can use this for wicked purposes. In the form of a crow, a
wicked person can spy and pry, learn things to use against

people whom they seek to blackmail or control.

Hopis have separate words for crow and raven. Crow is
angwusi, raven is *adoko*. There is a story about a little boy
who gets trapped on a cliff face and is rescued by Raven, who
flies to the frightened boy and tells him to climb upon his
back; after the boy is safely settled on the bird's strong back,
Adoko spreads his wings and carries the lad back to his home
village and safety. As a result of this incident, Adoko is sometimes called "Raven the Rescuer."

Crows are more common in Hopi country than are
ravens. Mountains such as Nuva-tukwa-ovi, Paiute (or
Navajo) Mountain, and Williams Mountain are havens for
both types of birds. Flagstaff, the city built where once the
Crow Clan farmed and hunted, is home to Crow and Raven
alike, as are the vast forests surrounding the city. Crows and
ravens abound in this region, perpetual home of the kachinas.

Epilogue

Among American Indian tribes it is said that the world we inhabit today is only one of many worlds, past and yet to come, worlds that existed before human beings were loosed upon the Earth, and that will exist after.

Whether Man will be part of these worlds to come is unclear, but one thing is certain: Great Raven and all of the natural powers that Raven represents always were and always will be, regardless of the role of Man. Raven loves Mankind, but Raven's world will continue long after Man's world is gone. The forces of Nature and the dance of the Universe are eternal.

The other day while walking across an open meadow, a raven flew over my head, called out, and cast his shadow over me. As I stood beneath his silhouette, with the shadow-form of his extended wings enveloping me and his raspy call echoing in my ears, I realized that, in one way or another, all of us live in the shadow of the Raven.

During the war in the Persian Gulf, human hands opened oil conduits and released millions of gallons of oily death into the gulf. Humans at war with one another over economic and political spheres of influence declared war on Raven's world as well. Sadly, human brutality is no longer limited to human beings; other children of Nature have been forced to pay the ultimate price for human foibles, human greed, and human selfishness.

In their arrogance, human beings have separated themselves from the Earth that gave them birth and gives them sustenance. In their ignorance, they set themselves apart from their natural brothers and sisters, the children of the Great Mother Earth, and announce that they alone are immortal, intelligent, and made in a god's image. The ancient Greeks had a word for this arrogance: "hubris," a type of pride that inevitably leads to destruction and divine punishment.

Raven is often interpreted as a manifestation of the Divine Earth Mother, and Crow is often depicted as a healer and messenger of many great gods, including Apollo. Apollo is an Olympian who brings retribution and justice to evil-doers. Raven and Crow are both affiliated with Lord Shiva and Lady Kali; when Shiva dances, worlds are created and destroyed and Kali is the only Goddess of the Hindu pantheon who demands blood sacrifice—crows are her emissaries.

Ultimately, the world will be cleansed, the natural order restored. And Great Raven will someday traverse a vast beach, hopping and flapping and stretching his beautiful wings. Perhaps, after pausing to eat some delicious tidbit on the shore to assuage his enormous appetite, Raven will feel bored and lonely. And then, Raven will bend down, and with his mountain-maker's hands, create new playmates, carefully crafting and sculpting new creatures, painting them in beautiful colors, building another world, again.

Afterword

arly one February morning in 1988, my husband and I were on our way for Saturday morning coffee when we saw a sad spectacle: an injured crow, dragging its left wing, dazed and walking in circles. A group of concerned crows, in all likelihood relatives and territorial clan members, surrounded him, making mournful sounds.

Though the morning was bright and clear, with a blanket of snow on the ground and a brilliant blue sky above, it darkened for us when we saw the suffering. We weren't sure what to do, as it is not always appropriate to interfere with the natural order of things. But we agreed that, at the very least, we should pick it up.

Both of us knew the inevitable result if the bird was left to his fate. He was pathetically vulnerable to cats, dogs, or people who might torment or kill him. Worse would be a lingering death from hunger and pain. It was obvious he couldn't fly. The crow, a creature of the air, had suddenly become earthbound.

We went back to the house and got a cotton sheet; I had done some work with birds and injured animals in the past

and knew that we needed to take precautions, not only for
the bird's protection and comfort but also for our own safety.
By the time we returned, the flock had dispersed and the
injured crow was no longer by the road. We were afraid that
the worst had happened.

As I carefully scanned the snow for tracks, I saw the im-
prints of crow feet, and we followed them. The bird was easy
to track because in addition to footprints, we could see the
mark made by his injured wing in the snow. We found the
bird hiding behind a woodpile, and threw the sheet over him.
He immediately turned on his back, with his claws facing out
in preparation for a fight, a typical defense reaction. Scooping
him up, we took him home.

I made an initial examination and determined that the
break, near the joint of the wing, was the type that usually
results in an amputation. As sick and wounded birds need to
be kept warm and protected, I found a cardboard box and
lined it with newspapers, and put a bowl of water, an ear of
corn, and some suet filled with insect parts inside the box.

I called the Flagstaff Game and Fish office, but as it was
Saturday, no one was there. The little fellow was still dazed,
but no longer in shock, and the injured wing needed immediate attention, so I called various local veterinarians; it was
already afternoon, and I was anxious. One close to my house,
a graduate of Washington State University's vet school (one of
the finest in the West), agreed to take a look at the bird.

The prognosis was not good. He explained that it was
likely that the wing would have to be amputated, but it was

worth trying to save it. We set the wing, using the crow's body as a support. As the doctor worked on the wing, the bird held my right index finger firmly in his beak and clung tightly to my left hand, his claws digging into my skin. He was so frightened and I felt so sorry for him that I didn't realize my hand was bleeding until after we had left the vet's office.

I asked the vet what to expect. His laughing response was, "Well, he's going to recover. He's a bit dazed now, but by this evening he will be rambunctious and obnoxious. You'll probably wonder whatever possessed you to stop and help him."

I have never regretted helping that crow. In the Navajo and Apache languages, crows and ravens are called *Gagee*, because that is the sound they make when they talk to people. I called my new charge "Hosteen Gagee," Mr. Crow.

Because of Gagee, I learned a lot about crows. I have always admired crows and ravens, and have known of their cleverness, resourcefulness, and varied mythological roles, but never fully appreciated their beauty and their intelligence until I lived with one.

I stayed with Gagee around the clock for four days. By the evening of the first day, he was hopping about, exploring the house. After sundown, however, he became sleepy and I put him in his box. As he recuperated, he spent his days in the garden, enjoying morning sunlight and afternoon shadow.

Gagee was a wild thing, unused to human company, and in the beginning, he was so shy that he would not eat if he saw me watching him. He had a favorite spot, a basalt rock beneath two aspen trees. Next to this rock was a deep snowbank where Gagee took his snow-baths, diving head-first into the bank. Morning, mid-day, and afternoon, I left fresh meat on the rock and allowed Gagee some privacy. After peering around to make sure that prying eyes weren't watching, Gagee ate the meat. He also had access to suet, seeds, gravel, chicken scratch, and water.

I read everything I could find about corvids and their nutritional needs. I learned that crows eat almost everything people do, and a lot of things they don't. Sunflower seeds, fresh pastries, bean sprouts, corn and popcorn, delectable giant mealworms, earthworms, nightcrawlers, and a special avian food mixture called Bird of Prey are high on their list of favorites. Dogfood is a good staple, and I started giving Gagee Purina Chewy Morsels Puppy Chow because of its calcium and high nutritional content; I felt he needed extra calcium and trace minerals to promote healing.

After the first few days, it became obvious that Gagee needed more protection than the sheltered garden provided. He was safe from wind and weather, but neighborhood cats, first intrigued by a wounded bird and then attracted by the bird's food, were climbing over the garden wall and into Gagee's new world. An aviary seemed like a good idea. After studying a number of designs, a suitable garden house was constructed.

Since the bird had only one functional wing, we had to be sure he had complete access to the three-tiered aviary as well as the normal protection from predators, a section for shelter from the elements, and privacy from prying eyes. Gagee's house had all of these features and more, including a blue spruce to hide behind, and which he used as an occasional ladder and feeding station. At the base of the tree, he developed a cache for his treasure trove.

We built a ladder connecting his sleeping and perch area with the ground, rungs spaced to crow proportions. (If any of the rungs slipped, Gagee would call us out from the house and peck at the damaged piece, and we would repair it.) On the upper level of his avian mansion, he had properly spaced rungs for walking and hopping, and branches for roosting.

After about three weeks in captivity, Gagee began to vocalize, announcing his presence and calling other crows and ravens. Gregarious, he shared the contents of his seed cups with local chickadees.

When spring arrived, Gagee enjoyed the garden with its shade, flowers, and variety of hiding places. He enjoyed hopping under our kayak and poking around. I gave him a wooden garden stepladder, formerly a plant-stand, for a perch. He enjoyed this ladder-perch and hopped up to the top rung to sun himself.

During the first few weeks of his convalescence, he constantly surveyed the garden, obviously scheming for ways to make his escape. Life with humans must have been confusing; perhaps he thought that if he could just get back into the air, his old life would be restored and he could return to flock and family. One afternoon, as Kevin made some improvements in the crow condo, I went shopping. When I returned, Kevin told me the story of Gagee's great escape. Poking around in the garden while Kevin was in the aviary, Gagee hopped from his favorite basalt stone to a garden chair and then jumped up into one of the aspens. Climbing up the aspen branches, he made a giant leap to the roof of the house next door and ran across it.

By this time, Kevin had seen what was happening and was himself scrambling up the garden fence and aspen tree in an attempt to catch the black bird with the white linen body sling. Moving rapidly across the length of the huge house, Gagee reached the roof's highest point. He spread his one good wing and made a magnificent leap. . . and sank like a stone, landing with a thud in the neighbor's backyard. Undaunted despite the hard landing, he scrambled for cover. At this point, he was easily caught and returned to the garden.

By the time I got home, Gagee was ensconced in a corner of the aviary, turning angry glares towards Kevin. His feathers were ruffled, and he was mad. The old saying "mad as a wet hen" came immediately to mind. After a rather less-hostile glance in my direction, he returned to glaring at the one who (he felt) had interfered with his escape. After that experience, Gagee apparently realized that he could not fly and did not try to escape again.

Despite our efforts, bone necrosis set in, and in early June, it became obvious that the wing had to go. Gagee was given antibiotics the evening before the procedure and spent the night at the vet hospital. The next morning, isofluorine, an effective and comparatively safe anaesthetic for birds, was administered and the damaged wing was removed. He was very unsteady when I brought him home, and I held him in my lap and stroked his head, neck, and beak. Even though I knew we had done all we could, and that he had been given proper nourishment and was strong and prepared for the ordeal of surgery, I couldn't help but regret that he would never fly and live a free life again.

After another period of recuperation, the work of rehabilitation began. From the beginning, Gagee courageously faced the challenge of regaining balance with only one wing. At first he was awkward, but as I worked with him, he became as graceful with one wing as he had been with two. He did not vocalize for three weeks after his surgery, however, and that worried me. But, as he recovered, he resumed his happy noisiness.

Soon after his recovery, Kevin bought him a beautiful ceramic Italian bird-bath, which made Gagee very happy. Every morning, Gagee waded into his imported tub and took a true bath. Gagee was also a successful worm rancher. During warm months, he pushed back a small log and foraged for fresh earthworms under the log base. When he had eaten all he wanted, he carefully pushed the log back in its original position. He hid favorite things behind the spruce tree, and whenever he felt shy, he would hide himself behind it, too.

He had other occupations as well. I bought him a toddler's "busy box," with a plastic tortoise-and-hare race, a bell, a red rubber bulb (which he promptly tore open and used to cache food), a shiny metal mirror in which he admired himself, a telephone dialing base, and a multicolored ball to push.

Because we wanted to be sure that he always had fresh

water, and weren't satisfied with the bird bath and his plastic water cups, we tried a variety of containers, including a water bottle normally used for rabbits. A clear-plastic-encased metal tube connected the body of the bottle to the water spout. Gagee was enraptured with this metallic silver spout. Although he learned to drink water from the tube, he really wanted the silver tubing—he wanted to possess the shiny object. One summer morning, he started pecking at the plastic that held the metal. Crows are persistent, as Gagee clearly demonstrated. After his morning bathing, eating, and playing routine, Gagee pecked, diligent in his determination to obtain the coveted metal spout. Finally, after two weeks of determined pecking, he succeeded in separating the metal tube from the bottle. He took it in his beak and hopped in triumph around the aviary, parading his treasure throughout all three levels of his house. When not playing with the spout, he hid it with his other valuables at the base of his spruce tree.

Gagee was a fabulous mimic. He barked like a dog, he chirped like a robin, he sang along with music boxes and ice-cream truck jingles, combining neighborhood sounds with his established crow vocalizations. After being together for two years, he sidled up to me and said "hello-hello-hello," sounds uttered from deep within his throat. It became his favorite greeting for me.

Gagee was aware of almost everything that occurred in our neighborhood. Whenever he became bored with his toys or the aviary, he entertained himself by spying on the girls next door. The cedar garden fence has small notches in it, just the right size for prying crow eyes. He would walk up to a notch, lean into it, and spy through this convenient peep-hole. Paki, one of our neighbors, is a graphic artist. After she became aware of Gagee's interest, she moved her drawing table over to a picture window facing the garden so Gagee could watch her better. Paki's dog Yodi also took an interest in Gagee, an interest which was reciprocated.

Despite our rapport, Gagee seemed to long for the company of other crows. After he had fully recovered from his surgery and was obviously going to be alive for a long time, I decided it was time to notify local officials to find out how I could obtain a non-releasable bird permit so that he would be legally protected. Our state Game and Fish officer explained that only if the federal Fish and Wildlife Service (whose regional office was in Albuquerque, New Mexico) approved my request for a humane federal permit would the State of Arizona grant me one. He said he knew of no one who had ever received such a permit. But he also admitted that he knew no one who had ever tried to obtain a permit. The intricacies of federal regulation regarding protected bird species have already been detailed in this book, and as the reader may have already surmised, I learned about the maze of rules and requirements the hard way.

My initial request for a federal humanitarian permit was denied because a local federal district supervisor has a policy of denying all humanitarian permits, despite guidelines outlined by federal regulations. Because I wanted Gagee out of harm's way, I contacted a friend in Window Rock, the curator of the Window Rock zoo, Dr. Loline Hathaway, and asked her if she could care for him. She agreed and sent two Navajo Nation Rangers to transport Gagee to Window Rock.

Before Gagee left, I visited a rehabilitation center in Verde Valley, Arizona, where there was a juvenile one-winged crow from California, named Tina by the staff, who would be making the trip to Window Rock with him. In Window Rock, they joined a one-winged raven. Gagee and Big Raven became friends. Tina, in addition to having only one wing, apparently had other socialization problems. Gagee and Big Raven became co-rulers of the roost at Window Rock, and kept an eye on Tina, who never interacted well.

Gagee was no longer lonely for other birds—he now had a real corvid family. It was better than anything I or Arizona Game and Fish could provide, so Gagee is still in Window Rock, safe and happy. I miss him, but his life and security were the reasons I picked him up on that February day. Together, we succeeded in his rehabilitation.

I am now acquiring additional training, specializing in corvids. They are so adaptable that their rehabilitation is much different than that of other songbirds. Gagee opened doors for me to the Bird People that I had never before considered. I will always remember and love Gagee, his courage, and his humor. I will remember him as Gagee the Warrior.

Annotated Bibliography
and Source List

A variety of sources, including published books and reports and interviews, were used in the research for this project. Although there is a great body of work on the subject of ravens and crows, sources for this study were restricted to those dealing with North American crows and ravens and Native American–related issues.

My studies of Greek and Roman mythology, Celtic and European stories, and formal training in Native American culture provided the basis for this research. These investigations were complemented and extended by friendships with Salishan, Nez Perce, Blackfoot, and Absorka individuals, who told me stories and how to care for injured birds.

Also referenced are a few children's books, not because I quoted from them but because they demonstrate in very clear ways the traditionally held perspective of Crow and Raven in other cultures and societies.

Published Sources

BLANCHET, FRANCIS NORBERT. *Historical Sketches of the Catholic Church in Oregon.* Edited and with an introduction by Edward J. Kowrach. Fairfield, Washington: Ye Galleon Press, 1983. Adventures of the Jesuits in the Louisiana Purchase territories. Interesting perspectives on the relationship between the Church and the Society of Jesus, as well as Catholic European missionary attitudes towards Indians and Protestant missionaries in the Oregon Country.

BYERS, PETE. *Crow Tamer Handbook.* Noble County, Ohio: Seneca Lake Bird and Field Naturalists Club, 1990. In what the author proclaims as "the first book ever written on this subject," the world of the amateur ornithologist is explored. Byers is an accomplished crow tamer, and the observations in this small paperback monograph are invaluable. The inclusion of a disclaimer—"liability for any loss or risk, personal or otherwise, resulting directly or indirectly from the use, application or interpretation of any of the contents of this book"— was wise, as snatching baby crows and ravens from their nests is illegal in the United States. I was very uncomfortable with the section on crow-killing, as well—hunting crows is not a worthy occupation. Still, Byers seems to love crows and knows a great deal about them.

CAMPBELL, JOSEPH. *The Masks of God: Primitive Mythology.* New York: Penguin Books, 1969. Enlightening but dated essays on comparative religion.

DEWEY, JENNIFER OWINGS. *Clem, the Story of a Raven.* New York: Dodd, Mead & Company, 1986. The adventures of a much-loved raven, saved from certain death after being blown from his nest in a New Mexico spring storm. A story of bonding between a raven and his human family.

HARRIS, CHRISTIE. *Raven's Cry.* New York: Atheneum, 1967. A fictionalized account for children about Haida life and the contact with Europeans that forever changed their world.

HEINRICH, BERND. *Ravens in Winter.* New York: Summit Books, 1989. The story of a dedicated ornithologist who endured the deep cold of Minnesota winters to study ravens, and his surprising discoveries about cooperative juvenile raven behavior.

KILHAM, LAWRENCE. *The American Crow and Common Raven.* College Station, Texas: Texas A & M University Press, 1989. Destined to be a classic in crow and raven studies, this book reveals the family lives of crows living in a world relatively free from human intrusion.

LA BARRE, WESTON. *The Ghost Dance.* New York: Dell Publishing, 1972. An interesting collection of ideas on religion, psychiatry, philosophy, and societal identity. In addition to maintaining that religion is the Ghost Dance of a traumatized society, La Barre theorizes about the many destructive mechanisms he feels are inherent in organized religion.

LOPEZ, BARRY H. *Of Wolves and Men.* New York: Scribners, 1978. One of Lopez's best works, this is a valuable resource leading to the works of other writers and naturalists as well as giving insight into wolf-raven cooperation.

LORENZ, KONRAD Z. *King Solomon's Ring.* Foreword by Julian Huxley. New York: Harper & Row, 1952. A beautiful book by the foremost naturalist of our century, this is a collection of essays spanning three decades in the life of a man who needed no magic ring to talk to and understand animals.

MAUD, RALPH. *A Guide to British Columbia Indian Myth and Legend.* Vancouver: Talonbooks, 1982. An exciting and well-written history of myth-collecting in British Columbia and a survey of published texts. An invaluable bibliographic tool.

MELZACK, RONALD. *Raven, Creator of the World.* Boston: Little, Brown and Company, 1970. Eskimo stories about Raven, as semi-divine folk hero and as eternal creative presence.

MOONEY, JAMES. "The Ghost Dance Religion and the Sioux Outbreak of 1890." (14th Annual Report, Bureau of American Ethnology, part 2, 1896). A masterpiece of human observation and compassion, this work fully explains the history and motivations behind the Father's Dance and the universal human dream of revitalizing the world and bringing to it justice and a restoration of the natural balance.

_____. "Myths of the Cherokee and Sacred Formulas of the Cherokee." From the 19th and 7th Annual Reports of the Bureau of American Ethnology, Reprint. Nashville: Charles and Randy Elder, Booksellers, Published in collaboration with Cherokee Heritage Books, an Educational Program of the Museum of the Cherokee Indian and the Qualla Arts and Craft Mutual of Cherokee, North Carolina, 1982. Much of this material was first recorded by Cherokee elders in their own language. Mooney spent time with them from 1887-1890. He visited with those who never left the mountains and with those who walked the Trail of Tears and settled in Indian Territory. Ancestors of former head of the United States Bureau of Indian Affairs, Ross Swimmer, were major contributors to Mooney's study.

MECH, L. DAVID. *The Wolf: The Ecology and Behavior of an Endangered Species.* New York: Natural History Press, 1970.

_____. *The Wolves of Isle Royale.* Washington, D.C., United States Department of the Interior, Fauna series 7, 1966. Two works by the definitive wolf ethologist, in which cooperation between wolves and ravens is discussed.

NELSON, EDWARD WILLIAM. *The Eskimo About Bering Strait.* Washington, D.C.: Smithsonian Institution Press, 1983. Originally published in 1899. Nelson made extensive ethnographic and natural history observations among Raven's people in the Arctic regions.

NELSON, R. K. *Make Prayers to the Raven: A Koyukon View of the Northern Forest.* Chicago: University of Chicago Press, 1983. In this beautifully written book, Nelson presents a sensitive portrayal of life among the Koyukon people.

NEQUATEWA, EDMUND. *Truth of a Hopi*. Reprint. Flagstaff, Arizona: Northland Press in cooperation with the Museum of Northern Arizona, 1967. This compilation of Hopi origin, migration, and European contact stories recounted by a priest of the One Horn Society of Second Mesa offers insight into the heart of Hopi identity. Hopi priests indicated that the Crow/Kachina clans originated at the base of the San Francisco Peaks, and Nequatewa's work provides further documentation.

ROBINSON, GAIL. *Raven the Trickster*. New York: Atheneum, 1982. A charming collection of standard Canadian and Northwest Coastal raven tales, this book is a fine piece of children's literature; its only flaw is that no tribal sources or origins are cited.

SELTICE, JOSEPH. Saga of the Coeur d'Alene Indian Nation. Unpublished notes and manuscript, private collection, Spokane, Washington.

STERN, PHILIP DOREN, ed. *The Portable Poe*. Reprint. New York: Penguin, 1987. A comprehensive and easy-to-carry Poe collection, with an interesting introduction by the editor.

Interviews with Author

Many Native Americans interviewed for this project asked that their names not be used, a cultural norm for many tribes, especially those of the Southwest. Others are already in the public eye—politicians, artists, and carvers—and therefore do not mind if they are credited for their contributions. Among many Northwestern tribes, a person may tell you a story and then say, "This is all I know about that. . . and now I will give this story to you." In this event, a very special gift has been given. Stories, dance regalia, and songs are viewed by many tribal peoples as property, and the giving of them is an honor to the recipient.

ANGLO-AMERICAN

DR. LAWRENCE KILHAM, October 1990 , Lyme, New Hampshire

ROBERT DELLWO, ESQ., October 1990, Spokane, Washington

ANGLO-CANADIAN

KEVIN NEARY, September 1990, Royal British Columbian Provincial Museum, Victoria, British Columbia

ANGLO-CHOCTAW

PHYLLIS HOGAN, series of interviews, 1981-1991, Flagstaff, Arizona

APACHE

DON DECKER, coffee house interviews, winter 1991, Flagstaff, Arizona

CELTO-CANADIAN

OWEN BRANDON, September 1990, Victoria, British Columbia

CHEROKEE/SENECA

MEDICINE GRIZZLY BEAR (Bobby Lake), October 1990, Spokane, Washington

EAST INDIAN (VEDIC)

MADAME INDIRA JOSHI, February 1991, San Francisco,California

HOPI

VERNON MASAYESVA, fall and winter 1990-1991, Flagstaff, Arizona

STANLEY BAHNIMPTEWA (Oraibi Kikmongwi), winter 1991, Oraibi, Arizona

CALEB JOHNSON, spokesman for Oraibi Kikmongwi, fall and winter 1990-1991, Oraibi, Arizona

Various members of One Horn Society and Flute societies of Second Mesa, Hopi Reservation, Arizona

KWAKIUTL
GEORGE TAYLOR, October 1990, Victoria, British Columbia

LAKES BAND OF NORTH CENTRAL WASHINGTON
KAYE HALE, October 1990, Museum of Native American Cultures, Spokane, Washington

LOWER COAST SALISH
CHARLES ELLIOTT, October 1990, Salish Reserve, Vancouver Island

MICMAC
RUSSEL BARSH, September 1990, Seattle, Washington

NAVAJO
MILLER NEZ, series of discussions and interviews, 1981-1983, Navajo Reservation, Arizona
Various traditional people from White Cone, Big Mountain, Chinle, and Teec Nos Pos, Arizona, regions

SAMISH
MARGARET GREEN (Tribal Chairwoman), September 1990, Samish Tribal Offices, Anacortes, Washington

SNOHOMISH
JACK KIDDER, September 1990, Snohomish Tribal Headquarters, Anacortes, Washington

Index